Cambridge Elements

Elements in Christian Doctrine
edited by
Rachel Muers
University of Edinburgh
Ashley Cocksworth
University of Roehampton
Simeon Zahl
University of Cambridge

A SENSE OF THE DIVINE

An Affective Model of General Revelation from the Reformed Tradition

N. Gray Sutanto
Reformed Theological Seminary

CAMBRIDGE
UNIVERSITY PRESS

Shaftesbury Road, Cambridge CB2 8EA, United Kingdom

One Liberty Plaza, 20th Floor, New York, NY 10006, USA

477 Williamstown Road, Port Melbourne, VIC 3207, Australia

314–321, 3rd Floor, Plot 3, Splendor Forum, Jasola District Centre,
New Delhi – 110025, India

103 Penang Road, #05–06/07, Visioncrest Commercial, Singapore 238467

Cambridge University Press is part of Cambridge University Press & Assessment,
a department of the University of Cambridge.

We share the University's mission to contribute to society through the pursuit of
education, learning and research at the highest international levels of excellence.

www.cambridge.org
Information on this title: www.cambridge.org/9781009527880

DOI: 10.1017/9781009527910

First published 2025

A catalogue record for this publication is available from the British Library

ISBN 978-1-009-52788-0 Hardback
ISBN 978-1-009-52789-7 Paperback
ISSN 2977-0211 (online)
ISSN 2977-0203 (print)

Cambridge University Press & Assessment has no responsibility for the persistence
or accuracy of URLs for external or third-party internet websites referred to in this
publication and does not guarantee that any content on such websites is, or will remain,
accurate or appropriate.

For EU product safety concerns, contact us at Calle de José Abascal, 56, 1°, 28003
Madrid, Spain, or email eugpsr@cambridge.org

A Sense of the Divine

An Affective Model of General Revelation from the Reformed Tradition

Elements in Christian Doctrine

DOI: 10.1017/9781009527910
First published online: April 2025

N. Gray Sutanto
Reformed Theological Seminary

Author for correspondence: N. Gray Sutanto, gsutanto@rts.edu

Abstract: How should one make sense of the Christian confession that God has instilled a "sense of divinity" in every person? While other approaches have identified the sense with a perceptual or cognitive faculty or with the empirical reports of theistic belief, this Element advances an affective model of general revelation, which draws from the writings of the neo-Calvinist branch of the Reformed tradition. The author argues that the sense of divinity refers to an implanted "feeling of divinity," a sensus numinis, and that this model makes better sense of the Christian witness, theologically reorients the empirical findings from the cognitive science of religion, and eludes influential objections against the doctrine of general revelation.

Keywords: general revelation, Herman Bavinck, Martin Heidegger, Reformed theology, Alvin Plantinga

ISBNs: 9781009527880 (HB), 9781009527897 (PB), 9781009527910 (OC)
ISSNs: 2977-0211 (online), 2977-0203 (print)

Contents

1 General Revelation: The Questions and Initial Statement

How should one make sense of the Psalmist's observation that "the heavens declare the glory of God" (Ps. 19:1)? Such a claim might lead to an amused reaction at best or outright confusion; after all, there appears to be a diversity of religious beliefs, and it is less than apparent that beliefs in the God described by the Psalmist in particular are prevalent. But the Psalmist goes on: this creational speech, apparently, reaches "the end of the world," and, like the sun, "nothing is hidden from its heat" (Ps. 19:4, 6). Paul, in the book of Acts, observes that God "did not leave himself without witness, for he did good by giving you rains from heaven and fruitful seasons, satisfying your hearts with food and gladness" (Acts 14:17).

In a seminal passage, Paul then observes that God has revealed himself so clearly through creation that none can be excused by claiming ignorance:

> For the wrath of God is revealed from heaven against all ungodliness and unrighteousness of men, who by their unrighteousness suppress the truth. For what can be known about God is plain to them, because God has shown it to them. For his invisible attributes, namely, his eternal power and divine nature, have been clearly perceived, ever since the creation of the world, in the things that have been made. So they are without excuse. For although they knew God, they did not honour him as God or give thanks to him, but they became futile in their thinking, and their foolish hearts were darkened. Claiming to be wise, they became fools, and exchanged the glory of the immortal God for images resembling mortal man and birds and animals and creeping things. (Rom. 1:18–23)

If the heavens declare the glory of God and all humanity has fallen short of that glory (Rom. 3:23), Paul argues, then the heavens are disclosing not merely "the eternal power and divine nature," but also the *wrath* of this God to all of humanity. Paul goes on to suggest that every human being knows the "righteous decrees" of God, for the "law is written on their hearts" (Rom. 1:32, 2:14). Though humanity knows God due to God's own self-revelation in creation (Rom 1:19, 21), humanity fails to acknowledge God as God and to give the glory that God deserves. It is folly to deny God's existence (Ps. 14:1).

These witnesses from Scripture have led much of the Christian tradition to argue that prior to, and in distinction from, the disclosure of verbal revelation from the prophets or apostles, God has revealed God's self in a universal way as the creator, sustainer, and judge of all that is not God. This teaching has come to be known and codified as the doctrine of *natural* or *general revelation*. God has *revealed* himself in a decisive way through the created order, such that all people, generally, are exposed to that revelation. As a result, all possess, in some way, a natural knowledge of God, or a "sense of the divine." General revelation is thus distinct from what has become known as *special revelation*, which has its focus on the particular redemptive acts and words of God throughout history, climaxing in the person and work of the incarnate Jesus Christ, and then recorded and communicated in the writings of Scripture. In special revelation, God condescends to speak in human language, accommodated to the finite capacity of human beings. If general revelation discloses God as creator, sustainer, and judge, special revelation discloses God as Triune and as humanity's redeemer. The one Triune God thus reveals himself by two means: one universal and nonverbal, and the other particular and verbal.

But this claim concerning the universality of the "sense of divinity" and general revelation has produced several perplexing questions. For instance, what exactly is the sense of the divine? Is it referring to a faculty that God has hardwired into every person, such that humans are predisposed to believing in God or is it referring to some sort of implanted knowledge? What does this sense of the divine have to do with the empirical data about the kind of religious beliefs that are (or are not) commonly produced? Is the sense of divinity merely a dogmatic claim, or does it also have observable empirical features? Further, the doctrine of general revelation has fallen on hard times even in the hands of Christian theologians of the past century; would not such a doctrine nurture a kind of epistemic hubris that allows for the projection of faulty human ideals unto the divine? Faced with such questions, some theologians have argued that one should jettison the notion that there is in fact a universal knowledge of God.

An appropriate model of general revelation should thus not only do justice to these seminal biblical witnesses, but also illumine everyday existence and address the important objections that have been raised against it. I argue that the affective model, drawn from the neo-Calvinist branch of the Reformed tradition, accomplishes exactly those aims. In this Element, I argue that the sense of divinity is the actual presence of a feeling of the divine, a *sensus numinis*, that God has instilled in every person. In so doing, I argue that this affective model makes better sense of the biblical and Christian witness, reorients the findings from the cognitive science of religion on religious diversity and cognitively natural theism, emphasizes the affective and phenomenological salience of the doctrine of general revelation, and eludes the influential theological objections against the doctrine.

After this first section, the second section sets the stage by observing some of the important passages in the Christian tradition on this doctrine and argues that, despite the presence of debates on how to construe the effects of and how human access to this universal revelation, there is at least a *minimal* doctrine of general revelation present in the Christian tradition. I thus locate the affective model as one stream within the live options on this doctrine.

The third section presents the affective model of the sense of the divine, drawing from the Dutch Reformed neo-Calvinist tradition's reflections on the teachings of Romans 1. I argue that the natural knowledge of God is most foundationally nonpropositional and affective, such that it produces a universal *feeling* or *affect* of the divine, or what Johan Bavinck calls the "sensus numinis" (J. Bavinck, 1940, 110; 1941, 15).[1] Though human reason may properly (or improperly) reflect on these affects as a second-order moment, the sense of the divine is not propositional awareness, nor is it about the activity of human reasoning, but is effected by a divine working alone on the human being and thus creating a "feeling of the divine" that precedes the activity of reason. I then compare this affective model to Alvin Plantinga's faculty-model of the sense of divinity, showing that the affective model does better justice to the biblical witness.

The fourth section sets the affective model in dialogue with some of the current findings in the cognitive science of religion on cognitively natural theism. In particular, I show that a strength of the model is in its emphasis that the sense of the divine is not dependent on empirical findings, and yet that it reorients how one might assess those findings. If the sense of divinity is a nonpropositional affect, then one cannot identify the result of the polls on "cognitively natural theism" with the sense of the divine, for propositional beliefs are second-order moments, and may be indicators of reason's fallenness in resisting to profess the unconscious awareness of divinity. This does not mean that there is no way to empirically attune ourselves to the sense of the divine, however. Here, I draw from Katherine Sonderegger's reading of John Calvin and Johan Bavinck to show that the model locates the affective salience of the doctrine of general revelation not in the area of reflected or professed propositional belief but in the phenomenological cares, or so-called magnetic points, that perennially draws the attention of agents. These cares in turn disclose our need for the Spirit's internal witness so that sinners would acknowledge the God they have long suppressed.

The fifth section clarifies the affective salience of the doctrine of general revelation by showing how one can know prior to and apart from

---

[1] I take propositions to be the meaning type that could be expressed by multiple linguistic tokens. Propositions are to language as concepts are to words. The proposition "The circle is red" can be expressed in multiple languages, for instance, while it is not reducible to just one linguistic token (the proposition is not primordially English, or Dutch, but is expressed by those languages). I take this to be an implicit argument for the reality of divine ideas as the archetype of human ideas. See Bavinck, 2019, 50–51.

propositions by offering a theological reinterpretation of Heidegger's phenomenology. I suggest that one can utilize his insights on nonconceptual phenomenological knowing in service of the affective model.[2] The theological deployment of Heidegger's phenomenology also serves to highlight three further benefits of the affective model: that it showcases the affective salience of the doctrine of general revelation, that it reorients the doctrine with a deeper, and more concrete, theological anthropology, and that it preserves the universality and efficacy of general revelation.

The doctrine of general revelation and its concomitant effects have fallen on hard times, however, and the sixth section further highlights the benefits of the affective model by showing how it addresses or evades some influential objections from Karl Barth, Klaas Schilder, and Ian McFarland.

The conclusion sums up the benefits of the model: that it does justice to the biblical witness, that it offers a way theologically to reorient our findings of the cognitive science of religion while preserving the affective salience of general revelation, and that it eludes the influential objections against the doctrine of general revelation that had been offered in the last century.

2 A Minimal Account: Historical Witnesses

To set the stage, there is, I suggest, a minimal doctrine of general revelation agreed upon within the Christian tradition, even while the term itself is not used by every thinker.

When Augustine inquires how it is that Plato "vehemently held" the truths of God's immutability, he speculates on whether Plato had read the revelation of the divine name in Exodus 3:14, but ultimately asserts that one need not "determine from what source he learned these things," for, appealing to Rom. 1:20, it was "more likely" that Plato knew about these divine realities from creational revelation (Augustine, 1993, VIII, 11–12). Augustine also appropriated Plato's doctrine of recollection into a theory of divine illumination: the mind understands reality not by recollecting "things previously known," but because "the nature of the intellectual mind has been so established by the disposition of its creator that it is subjoined to intelligible things in the order of nature, and so it sees such truths in a kind of non-bodily light that is *sui generis*" (Augustine, 2012, 12. 4. 12). Just as the eye sees through the sun, so does the intellect see through a divine presence and light, and is thus exposed to that light (cf. Copleston, 1950, 62–3; MacDonald, 2017, 356).

---

[2] So, Peter Joseph Fritz (2021, 309): "Counter-intuitive though it may seem, Martin Heidegger (1889–1976) provides positive impetus for fresh thinking on divine revelation." As I show, the affective model provides tools to theologically employ some concepts in Heidegerrian pheneomenology.

St. Bonaventure argues that the existence of God is a "foundation innate to the nature of man," not in the sense that humanity in itself knows God apart from revelation, but, citing Hugh of St. Victor, that it "was necessary that God present himself even while remaining hidden, lest if he were totally hidden, He should be totally unknown … this [God] does so that man's mind might be stimulated by what is known and challenged by what is Hidden" (Bonaventure, 1979, Q. 1. 1. Ad. 14). God manifests God's self in the human mind, such that "pure act" is that which "first comes to the intellect" (Bonaventure, 2002, 5. 3), and all nonbeing and potential being are rendered intelligible through the mind's acquaintance with the divine being. As a commentator clarifies, it is not that God is the first *explicit* object of the intellect, but that God is already *implicitly* known in every act of the intellect (Case, 2021). Appealing to John 1:9, Bonaventure argues that it is through the presence of this light that all other things are known (see also Webster, 2012, 171–92).

Thomas Aquinas, who displays a deeper emphasis on Aristotelian empiricism, argued that creatures are known first, and that the agent intellect abstracts intelligible species from sensible realities.[3] For Aquinas, Romans 1:19 implies that God can be known by natural reason (Aquinas, 1968, q. 12, a. 12), in the sense that God may be known as the cause and influence of creatures but not as the first thing known. It is implanted in us to know God "in a general and confused way," but "not to know absolutely that God exists" (Aquinas, 1968, q. 2, a. 1). God is the cause of our knowledge, "not as if He were the first known object, but because He is the first cause of our faculty of knowledge" (Aquinas, 1968, Q. 88, a. 3).[4] To put it another way, if Bonaventure emphasizes that God is that which first comes to the intellect because "God has shown it to them" (Rom. 1:19), Aquinas emphasizes that this revelation is "in the things that have been made" (Rom. 1:20). It follows, for Aquinas, that sacred doctrine is necessary, "because the truth about God such as reason could discover, would only be known by a few, and that after a long time, and with the admixture of many errors" (Aquinas, *ST* I, q. 1, a. 1).

---

[3] The differences between Aquinas and Bonaventure on the natural knowledge of God and divine illumination have been well documented. See Marrone, 2001; Cullen, 2006, 62; Schumacher, 2011, 176; Vater, 2022, 272–273.

[4] Aquinas's comment on John 1: 9 is apropos: "For when the Evangelist says, he *enlightens every man*, this seems to be false, because there are still many in darkness in the world. However, if we bear in mind these distinctions and take 'world' from the standpoint of its creation, and 'enlighten' as referring to the light of natural reason, the statement of the Evangelist is beyond reproach. For all men coming into this visible world are enlightened by the light of natural knowledge through participating in this true light, which is the source of all the light of natural knowledge participated in by men." Aquinas, 1980, 1. 129.

God thus reveals in sacred doctrine not merely truths that surpass reason, but also those truths discoverable by reason.

While the Reformed tradition has been charged with being rather double-minded about whether it affirms the possibility and positive status of the natural knowledge of God, the magisterial and orthodox Reformed theologians histor-ically continued to reflect on the implications of Romans 1 fruitfully (Manning, 2013, 197–8). The so-called "Reformed objection to natural theology" is not so much due to their rejection of God's revelation in creation but due to their deep consideration of the dynamic of "knowing" and "suppressing" that one sees in the Pauline text.

The important and influential passage on the "sense of the divine" comes from Calvin's *Institutes*:

> Men of sound judgment will always be sure that a sense of divinity which can never be effaced is engraved upon men's minds. Indeed the perversity of the impious, who though they struggle furiously are unable to extricate themselves from the fear of God, is abundant testimony that this conviction, namely, that there is some God, is naturally inborn in all, and is fixed deep within, as it were in the very marrow. . . . I only say that though the stupid hardness in their minds, which the impious eagerly conjure up to reject God, wastes away, yet the sense of divinity, which they greatly wished to have extinguished, thrives and presently burgeons. From this we conclude that it is not a doctrine that must first be learned in school, but one which each of us is master from his mother's womb and which nature itself permits no one to forget, although many strive with every nerve to this end. (Calvin, 1961, I. 3. 3.)[5]

I shall return to this important passage later, but for now, it suffices to note that for Calvin, the "sense of divinity" is "inborn" in all, and "presently burgeons," despite the attempts of sinful humanity to extinguish and suppress that sense. The sense of the divine is, Calvin argues, implanted in each human mind, not a faculty of the soul, learned in school, or gained by discursive reasoning (cf. Dowey, 1994, 51; Sonderegger, 2021, 393–394).

Franciscus Junius, along with other theologians from the period of Reformed orthodoxy, calls this revelation of God from creation "natural theology" and enfolds it as a subset of revealed theology (Junius, 2014, 136, 141). He argues that "natural theology is that which proceeds from principles that are known in relation to itself by the natural light of the human understanding, in proportion to the method of human reason," and, simultaneously, that "Paul argues that a shared intuition concerning God had been impressed upon them all" (Junius,

---

[5] For more on Calvin and the knowledge of God in historical and theological context, see Sudduth (2009, 15–17), Dowey (1994), Van der Kooi (2005, 63–74), Steinmetz (1995, 23–29), and Sonderegger (2021, 393–394). On Calvin's method in context, see Muller (2000).

2014, 145, 148). Such a theology is, however, "veiled and imperfect" and needs to be perfected by supernatural theology (Junius, 2014, 147).

Francis Turretin observes that natural theology is "partly innate," for God implants "common notions," and "partly acquired (drawn from creatures discursively)" (Turretin, 1992, 1. 3. 4; see also Basil on "preconceptions," 2011, 1. 5). The mind of humanity, furthermore, is a *tabula rasa* "not absolutely, but relatively as to discursion and dianoetical knowledge … but not as to apprehensive and intuitive knowledge" (Turretin, 1992, 1. 3. 11). When humanity denies God's existence, then, it's not so much out of genuine "ignorance" but due to "perverseness" (Turretin, 1992, 1. 3. 14.).

Petrus Van Mastricht continued to uphold an "inborn or innate knowledge, which freely comes into existence without reasoning, about which the apostle speaks in Romans 1:19," and an "acquired knowledge, which we obtain by discursive reasoning … Paul likewise speaks about this in Rom. 1:20" (Van Mastricht, 2019, 2. 55). The natural knowledge of God is not comprehensive, for such a knowledge belongs to God alone, but "apprehensive," that is, the knowledge *that* God is (Van Mastricht, 2019, 2. 55).

The *Synopsis of Purer Theology* argues that God reveals himself in creation, and that human beings are so exposed to that revelation that "the notion of God has been inscribed on the human soul as a first truth and a first principle" (*Synopsis*, 1. 6. 4.). Likewise, the Westminster Standards uphold that the "light of nature" manifests the divine attributes in a non-saving way (Westminster Confession of Faith, 1.1; Westminster Larger Catechism Q&A 2).

Junius's inclusion of natural theology as a subset of revealed theology is typical of the Reformed tradition, which rejects the view that natural theology is a purely rational enterprise divorced from special revelation or the whole system of Christian doctrine. Although, as one shall see, Herman Bavinck would later provide good reasons to prefer "general revelation" over natural theology as the more fitting term for this doctrine. Given that this is about *revelation*, after all, it would be a mistake to identify the older Reformed account with later treatments that tend to identify natural theology with purely philosophical proofs of God's existence (Muller, 2003, I. 283). This natural knowledge of God is suppressed by the unregenerate and leads to idolatry, whereas Christians, equipped with the spectacles of Scripture and the illumination of the Spirit, may indeed infer things about God from the created order, seeing creation for what it is, the handiwork of God. There is thus a false, unregenerate natural theology, and a true, illumined natural theology, both of which presuppose that God has revealed himself decisively through his created order.

Despite the varying emphases on the modes and access of the natural knowledge of God and its relation to human reason, there is, then, a minimal account of the doctrine of general revelation found in the Christian tradition as a sort of common ground. This minimal account is this: *God has revealed himself through creation sufficiently, universally, and non-savingly to humanity, such that humanity is without excuse in its failure to acknowledge God as its creator, sustainer, and judge.*

When one turns to thinkers from within the Dutch neo-Calvinist tradition at the turn of the twentieth century, represented by thinkers like Abraham Kuyper, Herman Bavinck, and Herman's nephew, Johan Bavinck, one sees great continuity with this minimal account and the Reformed inflections, along with a deepened reflection on what I call the "affective" dimensions of general revelation and a greater emphasis on general revelation being a *divine* work that precedes the activity of human reason. Kuyper, for instance, argues that "from the finite no conclusion can be drawn to the infinite, neither can a Divine reality be known from external or internal phenomena, unless that real God *reveals* Himself in my consciousness to my ego" (Kuyper, 1898, 343). The revelation of God in nature, thus impacts the "human heart"; it is "the steady impression on man's heart of God's omnipresent power" (Kuyper, 2015, 75; cf. Bratt, 2013, 209). Gleaning from romanticism, Kuyper located the effects of general revelation deeper into the affective.

Likewise, Herman Bavinck renders Calvin's sense of divinity as a "gevoel der godheid" (*feeling of divinity*; Bavinck, 1909a, 36–7), and Johan Bavinck refers to the same as a "sensus numinis," an intuition of the noumenal,[6] a working of God so strong in all living humans that it "penetrates into invisible backgrounds" and forms a "point of contact" for Christian evangelism (J. Bavinck, 1940, 110; 1941, 15, cf. Streetman, 1986, 104–25).[7] While the older Reformed tradition had already emphasized that God implanted notions that precede reasoned inferences from creation to God, these thinkers, as we shall further describe, located the effects of general revelation as further sedimented underneath notions, ideas, or propositions, that is, in affects, feelings, and intuitions.

It is from these sources that I draw an affective model of general revelation, and the advancement of this model is the focus of the rest of this Element.

---

[6] Cf. Edward Dowey (1994, 55): "We are here in the area of the truly numinous in Calvin's theology. This knowledge which is more than knowledge is a suprarational awareness of God's majesty to which man responds in fear."

[7] Unless otherwise noted, translations are my own.

3 An Affective Model of General Revelation

These neo-Calvinist thinkers provide the resources for a theological interpretation of "affects," or the "propulsive elements of experience, thought, sensation, feeling, and action that are not necessarily captured or capturable by the language of self-sovereign 'consciousness'" (Schaefer, 2015, 23).[8] Not to be confused with the conscious emotions elicited by one's attention on explicit objects, affects, or what Bavinck calls "feeling" (*gevoel*), are the intuitions that form and direct the embodied soul prior to explicit thinking or willing (Brock, 2020, 87). The sense of the divine is thus felt before it is propositionally cognized, and Johan Bavinck argues that humans "proceed as unknowing knowers" of the divine in their everyday existence (J. Bavinck, 2013, 284).

This section focuses on recovering Johan and Herman Bavinck's rendering of the sense of the divine, which is the result of God's general revelation. Their account enables one to recognize a kind of phenomenological knowing that precedes the use of linguistic or propositional media. It is a kind of "psychological" knowing, having to do with the Greek term "ψυχή," and is about the knowledge of the embodied soul, a knowing that informs and yet eludes conscious and attentive awareness. It is, as Herman Bavinck argued, "not a knowledge in concepts" ("*geen kennis in begrippen*"; Bavinck, 1897, 58), for it is not a knowledge of immediately formed propositions nor the result of reasoned reflection.

Johan and Herman Bavinck sketch this account of the sense of divinity on the basis of two features: a reading of Romans 1 that is attentive to the dynamic of "knowing" and "suppressing" and an affective theological anthropology.[9] Because Johan Bavinck has a sustained treatment of this Pauline text in his "Religious Consciousness and the Christian Faith," I shall start there before moving on to Herman Bavinck's reading of the same text, focusing on his language of *gevoel* (feeling). A sketch of Herman's anthropology that focuses on those features most relevant to grasping his account of the sense of divinity follows. Then, I turn to compare the affective model found in these authors with Alvin Plantinga's "faculty-model" of the sense of the divine.

3.1 Johan Bavinck on Romans 1

Johan Bavinck's reading of Romans 1 begins with the observation that Scripture appears to be paradoxical on the issue of general revelation: how is it that many passages of Scripture indicate clearly that many do not know God, and fall into

---

[8] On the "affective salience" of doctrine, see Zahl, 2015, and 2021. On Bavinck's anthropology and its interface with religious affect theory, see Sutanto, 2024.

[9] For more detail on Herman Bavinck's anthropology, see Sutanto, 2024.

idolatry, and yet that Paul speaks in Rom. 1:19–20 that *everyone*, in fact, knows God (J. Bavinck, 2013, 284)? This leads Johan to reflect on the tension between "knowing" and "suppressing." For Johan, a successful reading of the passage must do justice to both sides of that dynamic.

For Johan, general revelation is about making "evident" that God confronts every individual by way of a "voiceless speech," and this "*manifestio* constitutes the only point of contact in mission work" (J. Bavinck, 2013, 277). As a self-revelation of God, this is about an encounter rather than a "philosophical instinct": general revelation "must be understood more existentially" (J. Bavinck, 2013, 278). Johan thus argues that one must resist the temptation to resolve the tension between knowing and repressing by arguing that God's revelation is available in nature, and human beings are rendered "without excuse" because they fail to reason unto him. Such a move, Johan thinks, misses the force of Rom. 1:18–23: the knowledge of God is not a bare possibility conditioned upon whether one actively reasons properly from creation to God, but an *actual* fact that obtains in human beings because of God's action. He argues that one must "disentangle" general revelation from the "abstract philosophical accretions" that attended its articulations, and set it "in terms of biblical reality" (J. Bavinck, 2013, 238). Thinking, reasoning, observing, and conscious reflection are not "where God meets" humankind. Rather, "the meeting point of general revelation," Johan writes, is "first of all in the problems inherent in being human, that is, in being a fallen human being" (J. Bavinck, 2013, 279). The sense of the divine here is not incrementally gained by way of a process of reasoning, nor is it calmly contemplated as implanted propositions, but rather stirs up the heart of humanity as it resides in the primordial "given" of God's revelation. It does not mean that this sense cannot be reflected on or propositionalized (indeed, Paul has delivered precisely that in his description of the sense of the divine as involving the knowledge of God as creator and our guilt before God), but this is a secondary moment. For Johan, there is no circumstance in which human beings do not know God or do not enjoy his gracious, ever-present illumination. Failure to honor God or give thanks to him (v 21b) is *in the context of knowing God* (v. 21a). As I will elaborate, for Johan, human beings know God *affectively*, yet fail to express that phenomenological knowing *conceptually*.

Hence, the word "suppress" (vs. 18) here deserves close attention, for it cannot be a suppression that results in a lack of knowledge. Indeed, suppression presupposes the presence of that which is suppressed, and it occurs because humans feel their guilt and seek to hide (Rom. 1:18, 32). Suppression "need not be understood as a conscious action. It can develop in total silence in the human heart. I am inclined to understand this in the sense of repression, as the concept of repression has been developed in recent psychology. As a rule, repression occurs 'unconsciously, but that makes it no less real'" (J. Bavinck, 2013, 242). Humans are ethically responsible for what they do to this sense of the divine, and that unconscious act of suppression is always against the presence of the sense of the divine in the human heart:

> [S]uppression occurs so directly, so spontaneously, so simultaneously with the 'understanding and seeing clearly' that at the precise moment that people see, they no longer see; at the exact moment that they know, they already no longer know. Psychologically considered, this is in and of itself entirely possible ... In this connection one could even say that human beings, in being addressed by the world around them, always suppress an instance of their becoming aware as an instance in which God, who is present everywhere and in everything, presents himself and manifests himself to them in a very evident way. (J. Bavinck, 2013, 284)

At every point, one is exposed to general revelation, and at every point, one is reacting to it in unconscious ways: "God definitely reveals himself, but people immediately push it away, repress it, suppress it" (J. Bavinck, 2013, 285). It would be a mistake to infer here that J.H. Bavinck therefore diminishes the noetic effects of sin, as if his focus of repressing here renders sin's effects to be only primarily on the will, or that affirming the noetic effects of sin strongly means that one becomes unaware of God. Sin's effects on the mind and the will are so pervasive that the mind and will fail to apprehend and respond appropriately to what is internally known and acting upon them. To make sense of this paradoxical claim, J. H. Bavinck again turns to the reality of the unconscious:

> We need to keep a sharp eye on the fact that there is something distorted in the human condition. People have been resisting, suppressing. They have done so unconsciously. But they do so all the time, moment by moment *always unaware that they are doing so*. But at the same time, there is always a definite unsettledness deep within them as a consequence of that suppression ... the engine of this suppressing process runs noiselessly, but not so noiselessly that they never feel it running now and then and thereby realize that something is amiss in their lives. People play hide-and-seek with God. (J. Bavinck, 2013, 285, emphasis mine)

Johan Bavinck's reading discerns the possibility of a discrepancy between one's explicit professions and behavior and the internal conditions that might drive them. The sense of the divine, repressed in one's psyche, cannot be fully eradicated due to the persistence of general revelation. This dynamic of knowing yet repressing manifests itself in the existential feeling of unsettledness, and in the presence of idolatry – humans are religious creatures, made for worship of the divine, and when the sense of God as creator is repressed, the result is not a lack of worship but a misdirection of worship. As Johan says elsewhere, repression of the sense of divinity results in a "parasitic substitution" where one explicitly worships something else despite knowing the true creator in their unconscious existence:

> Man has repressed the truth of the everlasting power and the divinity of God. It has been exiled to his unconscious, to the crypts of his existence. That does not mean though that it has vanished forever. Still active, it reveals itself again and again. But it cannot become openly conscious; it appears in disguise, and it is exchanged for something different. (J. Bavinck, 2023, 117–18)

For Johan, this unconscious presence of the sense of the divine is that which forms the "point of contact" for Christian witness. The evangelist does not bring the word of special revelation to a blank canvas, so to speak, but to one who is already wrestling with God, its creator. This is a point of contact because only by being "illumined by the light of the gospel, they sometimes suddenly become aware of the horror of this suppressing process and realize that they have always known but have never wanted to know" (J. Bavinck, 2013, 285). Special revelation addresses directly the existential guilt and disposition to worship that the sense of the divine stirs up and brings to it the salve of forgiveness and atonement. The "sensus numinis" in humanity pits him against the "phanoresis" (manifestation) of God: "his creatures do not stand as one who no longer hears his voice" (J. Bavinck, 1940, 110). As I will describe in Section 4.2, this sensus numinis explains why it is that Johan argues humans are drawn to certain "magnetic points": the existential ways in which humans continue to elevate creaturely realities, feel angst and guilt for their sins even while they deny God's existence, desire solidarity with a greater whole, and so on.[10]

An analogy might help to capture the sense of Johan's emphases here. One might consider a family in which an estranged child, now an adult, receives daily texts from a sibling that their mother has been diagnosed with a fatal disease. Their mother has only about a few more years to live. These texts beckon the child to come home, but the child has so become accustomed to living on his own and ignoring the family that he refuses to respond or read the daily text messages. After a few months, the text messages are treated no longer as minor nuisances that require conscious deleting, but become ignored altogether, grouped with all of the other unread messages he receives, receding into the back of his subconscious. The child can go about his daily business

---

[10] Though J. Bavinck uses "sensus numinis" as a gloss of Calvin's "sensus divinitatis" and Romans 1:19–20 in the 1940 and 1941 works, he clarifies elsewhere that Rudolf Otto's deployment of the "sensus numinis" is different from Calvin's "sensus divinitatis," for one is not just aware of holiness but of a Holy *Someone* – of God himself. See J. Bavinck, 2013, 227–228, 274–275. I am grateful to Arthur Rankin for reminding me of this nuance.

without consciously thinking about the messages or his mother despite it being there in his subconscious – that is, of course, until that distant sibling shows up on his doorstep, forcing him to recall all the messages he had so successfully (in self-deception) coped with through suppression.

Similarly, for Johan general revelation is that visceral feeling or unconscious knowledge of God that all creatures experience by virtue of God's revealing act. One might no longer be attentive to it, but it can never be forgotten or eradicated and manifests itself in the ongoing idolatries and existential angst one feels. Certain prompts that occur within one's life, such as, perhaps, exposure to great beauty, a conversation about the meaning of mortality, or, attending a church service where the Word is preached, might cause the sinner to be confronted again with this sense of the divine that he or she has long submerged. For Johan, an emphasis on propositions and arguments for God's existence as a reading of Romans 1 domesticates the force of this Pauline passage and misses the concreteness of its teachings.

Johan Bavinck's reading of Romans 1 arms us with considerable benefits. Firstly, we can affirm that the knowledge of God is ever-present without denigrating the effects of sin that cause us to fail to apprehend God properly. Secondly, following from the first, we can maintain the paradox of knowing-yet-not-knowing that we articulated is the condition of sinners living in God's good world: we are, indeed proceeding as "unknowing knowers." Thirdly, we capture a deeper sense of sin's pervasiveness that goes beyond mere analyses of propositions and are thus enabled to describe it with empirical granularity.

Johan appeals directly to Herman Bavinck's *Dogmatics* as that which inspired his own view of the sense of divinity. From Herman, Johan was prompted to consider more clearly the locus of general revelation's impact (J. Bavinck, 2013, 274–5). It is to Herman's work that we now turn.

3.2 Herman Bavinck on *Gevoel*

Herman Bavinck's mature reflection of the effects of general revelation, as we saw, is found in his 1909 work *Magnalia Dei*, where he describes those effects as a "*gevoel*" of the divine. To understand the significance of that passage in context, one should situate it within his overall oeuvre. I will begin by observing his comments in *Dogmatics*, before turning to his 1908 *Philosophy of Revelation*, and then finally to the seminal passage in *Magnalia Dei*.

In *Dogmatics*, Bavinck argued that the terms general and special revelation do better justice to the teachings of Scripture over natural and supernatural theology (H. Bavinck, 2003, 311–12; Eglinton, 2012, 89). Though he recognized that the older Reformed theologians situated natural theology as a subset of revealed theology, he argued that the way in which natural and supernatural theology had been distinguished, especially in medieval scholasticism, tended toward an "absolute contrast," where God's revelation in nature and Scripture were related together mechanically, merely side by side, rather than organically. (H. Bavinck, 2003, 303–4). Furthermore, deploying the terms of general and special revelation emphasizes that *all* revelation is supernatural: "Scripture, though it knows of an established natural order, in the case of revelation makes no distinction between 'natural' and 'supernatural' revelation … Actually, according to Scripture, all revelation, also that in nature, is supernatural" (H. Bavinck, 2003, 307). If it is God "who reveals himself in his handiwork," it "presupposes that it is not humans who, by the natural light of reason, understand and know this revelation of God" (H. Bavinck, 2004, 74). Bavinck was concerned with maintaining the objectivity of revelation as a *divine* act and resisted its conflation with the activity of human reason or rational argumentation (H. Bavinck, 2004, 78).

To be clear, Bavinck affirmed with Reformed orthodoxy that human beings clearly perceive God's existence precisely because God's objective revelation is clear, and that, subjectively, human beings possess both the "capacity" and "inclination (*habitus*, disposition)" to conclude that God exists (H. Bavinck, 2004, 71). However, alongside these classical comments, Bavinck also emphasizes that God reveals himself *internally*, arguing that there is an "interior impact of revelation upon [humanity's] consciousness" that "precedes" both the implanted and acquired knowledge of God; there is, internal to the psyche, a "revelatory pressure" (H. Bavinck, 2004, 72–73). Hence, the distinction between innate and acquired knowledge of God needs to be clarified by the further emphasis that even the innate knowledge of God is, in a sense, acquired, for "God's revelation precedes both":

> And humans, having been created in the divine image, were gifted with the capacity to receive the impressions of this revelation and thereby to acquire some sense and knowledge of the Eternal Being. The innate knowledge of God, the moment it becomes cognition and hence not only cognitive ability but also cognitive action, never originated apart from the working of God's revelation from within and without, and is to that extent therefore acquired. (H. Bavinck, 2004, 73)

This is an important passage for the affective model, for, here, Bavinck distinguishes the knowledge of God from "cognitive ability" and "cognitive action" (cf. Brock, 2020, 252). As Bavinck writes in this passage, the impressions of revelation might "become" cognition by an act of the intellect. The activity of the intellect always presupposes that divine revelation "from within and without." Divine revelation is always from the outside, impinging itself in our consciousness, and the effect of that revelation is not reducible to explicit cognition, preceding it altogether.

When Bavinck finally turns to treat the proofs for God's existence, then, he argues that one should not treat these proofs in isolation from the Christian faith, nor as definitive demonstrations that serve as faith's preambles, but rather as a witness to one's religious consciousness. In other words, these arguments are mere witnesses to the reception of general revelation and the "feelings" that stem from them: "The situation is this: Faith attempts to give an account of the *religious impressions and feelings* [produced by general revelation] that we humans receive and carry with us in our soul" (H. Bavinck, 2004, 90, emphasis mine). God produces these religious "impressions and feelings," and these feelings, in turn, are worked upon by the intellect in order to produce a conceptualized articulation. Christians, armed with the spectacles of Scripture, are equipped to reflect on this revelation precisely because the articulated proofs witness "their own religious and ethical consciousness" (H. Bavinck, 2004, 91). Scripture articulates and connects with that which is already felt.

In the *Philosophy of Revelation*, Bavinck argues that "in self-consciousness, therefore, we have to deal not with a mere phenomenon but with a noumenon, with a reality that is immediately given us, antecedently to all reasoning and inference" (2018b, 53). He then draws from Schleiermacher to clarify the affective effects of this general revelation: prior to reasoning and active cogniz-ing, human beings immediately *feel* an absolute dependence on God (cf. Schleiermacher, 2016, §4. 2, §32–33). This is an implication of being a creature situated within God's handiwork:

> And this definite mode of being, most generally described, consists in a dependent, limited, finite, created being. *Before all thinking and willing, before all reasoning and action*, we are and exist, exist in a definite way, and inseparable therefrom have a consciousness of our being and of its specific mode. The core of our self-consciousness is, as Schleiermacher perceived much more clearly than Kant, not autonomy, but *a feeling of dependence*. In the act of becoming conscious of ourselves we become conscious of our-selves as creatures . . . We *feel* ourselves dependent on everything around us; we are not alone. (H. Bavinck, 2018b, 56–57; emphases mine)

Thinking, reasoning, and action are all embedded within a definite mode of existence as exposed to divine revelation. In Bavinck's reading, Schleiermacher is drawing from Augustine's turn to the self to show that the soul is pre-categorically aware of God's presence prior to active reasoning (H. Bavinck, 2018b, 55; see also Brock, 2020). Human reasoning, therefore, is always a second moment that itself presupposes an implanted phenomenological awareness, indeed, *an affect* – that God exists, and that we are absolutely dependent on him: "in self-consciousness both the existence and the specific mode of existence of the self and ego, are revealed" (H. Bavinck, 2018b, 58). It is precisely through interpreting the result of revelation as a preconscious affection that one should read Bavinck's provocative claim that revelation is the "secret of all that exists": "Revelation underlies all created being … the finite is supported by the infinite" (H. Bavinck, 2018b, 24). To identify the deliverances of human reflection with general revelation is thus to commit a fundamental category mistake for Bavinck, not to mention that it would hardly make sense of this passage, for it is impossible that human beliefs or activity underlie all created being. Revelation is the primordial environment, and that which affords or prompts human activity, and is strictly prior to it.

His comments in the 1909 text, the *Magnalia Dei*, which is an updated, more accessible synopsis of his *Dogmatics*, naturally follow from these broader and earlier developments in Bavinck's thought. Before describing the effect of general revelation as a "feeling of the divine," Bavinck appeals to the older doctrine of illumination that there is an "impression of the divine in us," which helps us recognize the divine impressions "outside of us," "just as the eyes allow us to see light and colors, and the ear which enables the hearing of sounds" (H. Bavinck, 1909a, 35). It was Calvin, Bavinck argued, who recognized this "feeling of divinity" (*gevoel der Godheid*), as it was taught by Paul in Rom. 1:20 (Bavinck, 1909a, 36). Bavinck went on to describe this feeling of divinity as a "feeling of dependence":

> In the first place, a feeling of absolute dependence is characteristic of it. Underneath the intellect and will, underneath our reasoning and action, there is in us a self-consciousness which is interdependent with our self-existence and seems to coincide with it. Before we think, before we will, we *are*, we *exist*. We exist in a *definite* way, and in indissoluble unity with this existence we have a *sense* of existence and a sense of existing *as* we are. And the core of this near identity of self-existence and self-consciousness is the feeling of dependence. In our inmost being, we are immediately, without benefit of reasoning, that is, and prior to all reasoning – conscious of ourselves as created, limited, dependent beings … humanity is a 'dependent' of the universe. And, further, he is dependent, *together with* all things, and dependent in an absolute sense, on God, who is the one, eternal, and true being.[11] (H. Bavinck, 1909a, 36)

---

[11] A parallel passage is found in Bavinck, 2022, 23: "The fool may say in his heart, 'There is no God' (Ps. 14:1), but deep in every human soul is the feeling of absolute dependence (*gevoel van volstrekte afhankelijkheid*) on an almighty power, a feeling (*gevoel*) of divinity – just as Calvin

While Schleiermacher posits the feeling of absolute dependence as the essence of religion and that on which dogmatics reflects, for Bavinck, the feeling of absolute dependence is an effect of general revelation, and that to which special revelation addresses, as given in the Scriptures. This feeling is concomitant with creaturely existence and is located in one's consciousness but apart from and "underneath our reasoning and action." In connection with Rom. 1:19–20, we feel ourselves dependent on God's eternal power, for we have the intuition that God is the creator. In conjunction with Rom. 1:32, we feel that we are guilty before God, for God is also the moral judge.[12]

In sum, the affective model of general revelation, which draws from the two Bavincks, renders the sense of divinity as feelings of the divine that are prior to and independent from human reasoning. Whether one describes this affective sense of the divine as a sensus numinis that is repressed (Johan), or a feeling of absolute dependence (Herman), both authors are clear that propositional or conceptual awareness is a secondary and derivative moment, not having to do with the reception of general revelation at its most basic level. The sense of the divine, then, just is the implanted affect itself; it presupposes that humans have the capacity to receive these affects, but it is not identified with those capacities for the affect is the result of a divine work. One might wonder how something can be meaningful or known prior to propositions, and I shall address this later by drawing some concepts from Martin Heidegger's phenomenology. Before that, however, it is helpful to further clarify this affective model by comparing it to the influential account of the sense of the divine by the philosopher, Alvin Plantinga, in order to show that the affective model does better justice to the biblical witness.

3.3 Alvin Plantinga's *Sensus Divinitatis*: A Faculty-Model

Plantinga's *Warranted Christian Belief* provides a seminal account of the sense of divinity that he draws from the works of both John Calvin and Thomas Aquinas. While Plantinga's epistemology of proper function is many-sided and his arguments touch on a variety of issues, from the nature of warrant, epistemic justification, and the noetic effects of sin, what's most relevant here is his description of the sense of the divine as a kind of cognitive faculty that is

---

called it thereby; also a seed, a principle of religion and morality." See also Dowey, who likewise connects Calvin sense of divinity to Schleiermacher's feeling of absolute dependence. 1994, 55

[12] Bavinck's location of the sense of the divine in feeling, underneath reason and the will, presupposes his account of the faculties of the human person. He argues that the soul has two faculties: the intellect and the will, but there are unconscious and conscious dimensions to both. "Feeling" has to do not with a third faculty, therefore, but with that intuitive knowledge prior to conscious thinking, and affirms that there is thus a "knowledge without concepts." For more on this, see H. Bavinck, (1897, 57–58, 82–83), and (2008, 186–187).

prompted, under the right circumstances, to produce theistic beliefs. The sense of the divine is an "input-output device," "the operation" of which is initiated by particular circumstances, such as the "perception of my guilt," exposure to the beauty of the Grand Canyon or a tiny flower, and so on (Plantinga, 2000, 174–175). The sense of the divine thus produces beliefs that resemble "perception, memory, and a priori belief"; it produces beliefs that are apprehended immediately, not inferred from other beliefs, and serves as "starting points for thought" – beliefs that are properly basic (Plantinga, 2000, 175–176). As Plantinga writes:

> The *sensus divinitatis* is a belief-producing faculty (or power, or mechanism) that under the right conditions produces belief that isn't evidentially based on other beliefs. On this model, our cognitive faculties have been designed and created by God . . . The purpose of the *sensus divinitatis* is to enable us to have true beliefs about God; when it functions properly, it ordinarily *does* produce true beliefs about God. These beliefs therefore meet the conditions for warrant; if the beliefs produced are strong enough, then they constitute knowledge.[13] (Plantinga, 2000, 179)

It is not that one needs to be aware that one is created with this belief-producing mechanism in order to produce warranted theistic beliefs.[14] Rather, it is simply that because one is created with this faculty, one finds oneself believing in a divine being, under certain conditions, just as one might produce a belief about the whiteness of the wall when the wall is perceived in front of one's self, or that our spouse is angry at us when we perceive his or her body language.[15]

When Plantinga turns to the noetic and cognitive consequences of sin to account for the presence of nontheism, then, Plantinga speaks about the malfunctioning of the sense of divinity. It no longer works as it should, and thus fails to produce beliefs in God as frequently or as strongly: "failing to believe in God is a result of some kind of dysfunction of the *sensus divinitatis*" (Plantinga, 2000, 184). Again, "failure to believe can be due to a sort of blindness or deafness, to improper function of the *sensus divinitatis*" (Plantinga, 2000, 186). This explains why it is that some believe in God and others do not: "The condition of sin involves *damage* to the *sensus divinitatis*, but not

---

[13] Plantinga repeats these descriptions in his *Knowledge and Christian Belief*, 2015, 36–37.

[14] Blake McAllister and Trent Dougherty (2019, 537–557), have shown that the sense of the divine, for Plantinga, need not refer to a sui generis religious faculty, but just is humanity's ordinary perceptual faculties that allow us to produce beliefs about God or "theistic seemings."

[15] Tyler Mcnabb's (2018, 22) description of Plantinga's epistemology is apt: "He argues that, if God exists, and if He has successfully constituted subject S's cognitive faculties in such a way that, when they are properly functioning in the environment for which they are meant, they would produce the belief that God exists, then S's belief that God exists could be warranted even apart from argumentation."

obliteration; it remains partially functional in most of us" (Plantinga, 2000, 210). It is the renewing work of the Spirit that repairs that sense of divinity, such that it can produce theistic beliefs again appropriately, under the right conditions.

Before we recognize the differences between Plantinga's and the affective model, it is worth noting that Plantinga's faculty-model of the sense of divinity is not altogether incompatible with the affective model I've described in Sections 3.1 and 3.2. The affective model does not deny the possibility of immediately formed apprehensive beliefs about God, or even that, as image bearers, humans may have the disposition, even propensity, to form theistic beliefs.[16] The affective model emphasizes, however, that the effects of general revelation lie prior to the formation of such beliefs. These affects of the divine might lead to an explicit articulation in the form of an immediately held belief, but need not rise to that level. As we saw, it is a knowledge without concepts, an intuitive, propulsive pull, sedimented in the embodied soul, which may manifest itself in a variety of ways: the instinct to worship, to prioritize some higher destiny, a sense of angst or guilt when having done something wrong, and so on.

The basic difference between the faculty-model and the affective one, however, is in the identification of the sense of the divine. The sense of the divine, for the affective model, is not a faculty, akin to one's perceptual faculties, though, as we saw, it presupposes that there are tacit dimensions in the knowing faculty, as in Herman Bavinck. The sense of divinity corresponds to the faculties of knowing (indeed, the tacit, nonconceptual, and unconscious aspects of knowing), but it is not identified with those faculties. The sense of the divine just is the sensus numinis (Johan), and just is the feeling of divinity, which concretely manifests itself as a feeling of absolute dependence (Herman). Because the sense of divinity is affective and instilled by divine agency alone (through creation), it would make no sense to describe this sense as malfunctioning or damaged due to sinfulness (for how can God or his activity malfunction?). Rather, sinfulness has caused one to misapprehend, repress, and suppress what one knows deep within; instead of acknowledging the God we feel, our explicit thoughts and directions manifest the heart as a "factory of idols" (Calvin, 1961, I. 11. 8). This repression is not reducible to inferring false beliefs about God, nor is it merely failing to produce immediate beliefs about God when prompted by the right conditions. It is a heart-wrestling, a sense of inner strife, akin to seeking to forget a long-repressed experience that may or may not

---

[16] For a comparison of Plantinga's and Thomas Reid's broader epistemology with Herman Bavinck's, see Sutanto, 2018.

be explicitly remembered, and which can only be relieved by the illumination of the Spirit, working with the redemptive word.

Plantinga's interpretation is, on one level, understandable, because "sense" is ambiguous. It can refer to the "sense of taste," for instance, and such a sense might be dulled if we had damaged our taste buds. He seems to be taking the sense of the divine in this way, and hence he argues that the *sensus divinitatis* can be damaged, thus failing to properly yield beliefs about God. But "sense" can also be taken as the content itself, as it were, and hence it is *of* the divine. It is in this latter sense that the Bavincks suggest that God himself has implanted a pre-theoretical awareness of the divine.

I suggest that the affective model is a better reading of Calvin's language and, correspondingly, of Paul's words in Romans 1 over Plantinga's.

Plantinga initiates his presentation of his model by referring to Calvin's words on the sense of the divine, which we saw as well at the beginning of this Element. The salient part of the passage is that Calvin describes the sense of divinity as "engraved upon man's minds," it can never be "effaced," though we struggle "furiously" to "extricate" ourselves "from the fear of God," and that it is "not a doctrine that must first be learned in school, but one of which each of us is master from his mother's womb and which nature itself permits no one to forget" (Calvin, 1961, I. 3. 3; see also Adams, 2001, 281–282). Plantinga suggests that this passage is "extravagant," and argues, tentatively, that what Calvin really means is that the sense of divinity is "a kind of faculty or a cognitive mechanism … which in a wide variety of circumstances produces in us beliefs about God" (Plantinga, 2000, 172). Plantinga then argues that Calvin cannot mean that the knowledge of God really is universal, and again wants to identify the sense of the divine with a mere capacity:

> It also sounds as if Calvin thinks knowledge of God is *innate*, such that one has it from birth, 'from his mother's womb'. Still, perhaps Calvin doesn't really mean to endorse either of these suggestions. The *capacity* for such knowledge is indeed innate, like the capacity for arithmetical knowledge. Still, it doesn't follow that we know elementary arithmetic from our mother's womb; it takes a little maturity. My guess is Calvin thinks the same with respect to this knowledge of God; what one has from one's mother's womb is not this knowledge of God, but a capacity for it. Whatever Calvin thinks, however, it's our model; and according to the model the development of the *sensus divinitatis* requires a certain maturity (although it is often manifested by very young children). (Plantinga, 2000, 173, emphases original)

Plantinga thinks that Calvin cannot mean that everyone has the knowledge of God, because, clearly, infants do not *really* know God, at least, not just yet. Just as the capacity for arithmetical knowledge is innate but the knowledge itself comes later, so it is with the capacity to form theistic beliefs. The capacity to form theistic beliefs itself is innate, but it takes a little maturity, through the right conditions, for that capacity to be actualized in the right way.

Though Plantinga admits that he is not ultimately interested in advancing Calvin's meaning, I suggest that Plantinga's reading here softens and domesticates Calvin's passage in a way that the affective model does not, precisely because it resists the identification of the sense with explicit thinking or reasoning.[17] Indeed, as Dowey has shown, for Calvin, the sense of divinity was not

> a special organ or faculty of the soul . . . and Calvin does not represent this as a formal possibility or precondition of knowing God. This is already *notitia*, knowledge, and indeed, religious knowledge. It is a material and existential concept describing an actual, vital knowledge relationship of the human mind with God. The *sensus divinitatis*, or *deitatis*, is not the product of ratiocination, such as we shall find in Calvin's analysis of the knowledge of God derived from external nature. (Dowey, 1994, 51)

For the affective model, the sense of the divine is not a faculty but is instilled by God himself; it is the *feeling* itself of the divine. It offers an alternative and more accurate reading of Calvin's passage. For the affective model, it is not impossible that infants know God, perhaps akin to the way in which infants recognize the voices of their parents, or facial expressions, even prior to the development of their cognitive faculties. If the sense of divinity is not a "doctrine learned in school," then no amount of "maturing" will have any effects on the presence of the sense of divinity, just as no amount of human repression will efface it either. Plantinga, it seems, presupposes an exclusively propositional model of knowledge (as warranted true belief) and imposes it on Calvin's text.[18]

Indeed, to identify the sense of divinity with human growth, human ability, or, indeed, a faculty of the human person is to confuse *revelation* (which is from God), and the human response to that revelation. Revelation presupposes that humans (as image bearers) can receive that revelation and later reflect on that revelation, to be sure, but revelation is a strictly divine work. The affective model emphasizes, therefore, that the feeling of divinity is indeed universal, but it is not, technically, "innate," but instilled or implanted, preceding even the formation of immediate beliefs. Everyone knows God, "because God has shown it to them" (Rom. 1:19). It has the benefit, over Plantinga's, to affirm the universality and efficacy that Calvin and Paul ascribe to the work of general

---

[17] It is for this reason that Jong, Kavanagh, and Visala (2015, 259) suggest that Plantinga's model is only "tenuously" related to that of Calvin's.

[18] Cf. Sonderegger (2021, 394).

revelation, refusing to exclude infants (and, one might suggest, the neurodivergent) from the feeling of divinity.

4 Reorienting the Findings of the Cognitive Science of Religion: Affect and Propositions

4.1 The Cognitive Science of Religion and "Cognitively Natural Theism"

The affective model does not merely do justice to the biblical witness over the faculty-model – it may also theologically reorient how one might consider the empirical findings associated with the sense of the divine from the cognitive science of religion. The affective model is a dogmatic account, to be sure, and its priority is to advance a model consistent with the biblical witness and Christian tradition and is as such not dependent on empirical results. Nonetheless, its strength is that it offers a more satisfying theological explanation of those findings, and in so doing we shall see that it addresses the vexed issue on whether the sense of the divine is to be identified with the reports concerning the most common theistic beliefs.

This first subsection surveys the empirical findings from the cognitive science of religion, along with two theological lines of responses to those findings: that the yields show that sin has often caused the loss of the natural knowledge of God, or that the findings depict for us a "cognitively natural theism" to be identified with the divine being disclosed in general revelation. The next subsection draws from Katherine Sonderegger and Johan Bavinck to show how the affective model rejects those two lines of responses and provides a more theologically satisfying reorientation to the empirical yields of the cognitive science of religion, while identifying and preserving general revelation's affective salience.

The cognitive science of religion is a subfield of cognitive science that studies the "mental processes that concern religious phenomena, such as religious experiences, beliefs, practices, and dispositions" (Van den Brink, 2020, 243; cf. Barrett, 2021, 519). One of the yields of this research is the demonstration that religious and theistic beliefs are formed with significant regularity, suggesting that the human brain has evolved in such a way that it is hardwired to produce such beliefs.[19]

---

[19] For more on the cognitive science of religion, see Van Eyghen, Peels, and Van den Brink (2018), McNabb (2018, 25–33), Barrett (2004), Clark and Barrertt (2011), and Clark (2018). For more on how Herman Bavinck's anthropology and doctrine of revelation might intersect with affect theory and the cognitive science of religion, see Sutanto (2024, chps. 3 and 4).

More specifically, practitioners refer to a Theory of Mind (ToM), which describes a cognitive bias that produces beliefs in supernatural agents and teleology. For instance, humans naturally believe that other agents act because of internal states of intentionality: Peter sees Susan hastily taking a bite of her sandwich, and immediately believes that Susan does so because she is hungry, or because she is rushing to a meeting, and so on. The ToM is also linked with an agency-detecting device. Humans seem hardwired to believe that certain occasions are linked with agency: that, say, the rain is here because something – or someone – out there is punishing me, or, that dinner on the table means that my spouse, who loves me, has prepared this for me. Aku Visala (2018, 105) observes that humans have also developed a ToM of higher orders, for we are able not just to detect what other agents seem to be intending in their actions, but also how those agents might perceive the way we intend certain acts, or how we might be perceiving *their* intentions, and so on. The ToM and the agency-detecting device thus also predispose humans to believe that supernatural agents are involved in everyday occasions: the traffic is smooth because God (or some deity) is blessing me, that I failed to get a promotion because I am receiving punishment due to my past wrongdoings, and so on.

As it turns out, therefore, religious and theistic beliefs are produced naturally by human cognition. Without argument or coercion, humans "appear to be naturally inclined to see the world as purposefully designed, *and* easily see an intelligent, intentional agent as behind this natural design" (Barrett, 2021, 524, emphasis original). This research has produced a bit of a double-edged sword with respect to the rational status of those religious beliefs. On the one hand, some might suggest that because humans are hardwired to produce beliefs in supernatural agents, this might well just be an evolutionary quirk, and a by-product that undermines their rational status (e.g., Dennett, 2006). On the other hand, however, these empirical findings seem to confirm the traditioned Christian claim that God has, indeed, revealed himself in creation. Many have thus linked these findings with Plantinga's faculty-model of the sense of divinity. Kelly Clark (2019, 72–73), for instance, suggests that these findings disclose that humans have a "God-faculty": "the cognitive science of religion suggests that we have a cognitive faculty that produces God-beliefs without recourse to argument."

Yet, things are not all that simple – as Clark himself is aware, the ToM and agency-detecting device seem to be producing a diversity of religious beliefs, all of which are context-dependent (cf. Barrett, 2021, 525, 528). They produce beliefs that not only confirm, but are also at odds with the traditioned claims from Romans 1. These involve beliefs that are not merely about a creator God who is holding creatures accountable for sin, but also about all sorts of anthropomorphic supernatural agents that are less metaphysically or ethically demanding than that of the almighty Creator depicted by Paul, beliefs that lead to other religions, and beliefs that fail to anticipate other Christian beliefs (Clark, 2019, 76).

Faced with these challenges, theologians have tended to produce one of two responses. The first response goes this way: given the diversity of religious beliefs, we should admit that the faculty that produces true God-beliefs is in fact malfunctioning due to sin – such that we often fail to produce beliefs in God, and perhaps that the noetic effects of sin mean that humans often fail to know God at all (e.g., Plantinga himself, as we saw in Section 3.3). A second response, however, is to identify the most common beliefs that have been reported from the cognitive science of religion with the output of general revelation. Launonen and Mullins (2021), for instance, have argued that the God of so-called classical theism, with its beliefs concerning divine atemporality, simplicity, and immutability, is a far cry from the empirical yields of the cognitive science of religion. They argue that proponents of classical theism risk denying the doctrine of general revelation given that these empirical findings show that the most common theistic beliefs have to do with divine beings that are larger extensions of human persons. For, if the doctrine of general revelation is true, it follows that humanity will produce theistic-tracking beliefs, and if the empirical yields show us that the typical theistic beliefs picture the divine being as "parts of the spatio-temporal universe; agents among other agents" (Jong, Kavanagh, and Visala, 2015, 251), then this must be the sort of God that general revelation discloses, so the argument goes. Launonen and Mullins, therefore, suggest that open theism seems to be the model of divinity most in line with the most common yields of the cognitive science of religion, and, therefore, with the divine being disclosed in general revelation: "Most believers fashion God in the image of man, the Creator in the image of a creature" (Launonen and Mullins, 2021, 8).

4.2 Locating the Affective and Phenomenological Salience of General Revelation

How does the affective model of general revelation address these findings of the cognitive science of religion, and the two lines of responses surveyed in Section 4.1?

First, the affective model resists the conflation of the professions of theistic beliefs reported by these empirical findings with the sense of the divine itself. The affective model argues that the sense of divinity produces a feeling of dependence on God that may or may not be articulated propositionally.

Conscious, deliberate reasoning or propositional formation are thus second moments that may or may not reflect those affects or unconscious knowledge. Both Plantinga's and Launonen and Mullins's responses presuppose the identification of propositional beliefs and the output of the sense of divinity, and thus suggest that either some humans may no longer have any knowledge of God (Plantinga), or that general revelation produces a picture of the divine being bound in space and time (Launonen and Mullins). However, the affective model suggests that the sense of divinity is not identical with the profession of propositions, and effectually persists *even if no one professes belief in God, indeed, even if the majority denies* God.[20] Thus, it would be a mistake to identify the results of the polls with the results of general revelation.

Katherine Sonderegger's observation concerning the distinction between Calvin's more phenomenological account of the sense of divinity and the products of explicit reasoning dovetails well with the affective model advanced here:

> On one hand, Calvin does not hesitate to say that human beings are 'naturally religious'; they are created with an ineradicable *sensus Divinitatis* that can only be stilled in the human heart by crude idolatry, perversity, and material greed. In moments of danger, seasons of trial and loss, the seed planted deep in the heart will spring up … In this way, an 'existentialist' or phenomenological account of human transcendence into God of the sort we find in Tillich or Rahner is not a foreign country to Calvinists. But on the other hand, Calvin does not hold, nor does the Reformed tradition as a whole, that God is a speculative concept available to the rational intellect, common to the human race itself. The nerve is cut to the kind of fundamental theology prevalent in Vatican I theology, and its famous and controverted 'natural knowledge of God'. (Sonderegger, 2021, 394)

There is thus a fundamental distinction between the "seed planted deep in the heart" that may "spring up," and the articulations of the "rational intellect." The result of the sense of divinity, as Calvin argued, was not an appropriate belief in God, for sinners "do not therefore apprehend God as he offers himself, but imagine him as they have fashioned him in their own presumption" (Calvin, 1961, 1. 4. 1.). Dowey thus summarizes that the sense produces in fallen sinners "the universality of religion, which because of sin means the universality of idolatry, accompanied by (2) the servile fear of God and (3) the troubled conscience" (Dowey, 1994, 53).

---

[20] Further, given a Reformed account concerning the unity of general and special revelation, Reformed theologians would insist that special revelation is needed for fallen humans to no longer suppress and thus confess aright what was disclosed in general revelation. See Bavinck (2003, 304).

Sonderegger continues to observe that, for God to be properly acknowledged, there must be a convicting of one's sins by way of the work of the Spirit that allows us no longer to suppress the sense but to recognize God: "God must be known, rather, through an awakening of one's conscience, a conviction of sin – to use nineteenth century parlance . . . or the 'inner testimony of the Holy Spirit' as the mere words of the Bible or the preacher becomes the Word of Life itself. This is the joining of reverence and gratitude, the knowledge of divine benefit extolled by Calvin in the *Institutes*" (2021, 394). The empirical yields of the cognitive science of religion, therefore, testify not so much to the content of the sense of the divine but to its suppression, as humans resist confessing that deep-seated affect that renders them accountable before God. Those who endorse both classical theism and the affective model could thus respond to Launonen and Mullins that the most common beliefs recorded in the cognitive science of religion disclose not so much the output of the sense of the divine but the idolatrous responses of sinners to that sense.

Hence, in distinction from Plantinga, proponents of the affective model would argue that it would be impossible for any human being to lose the sense of the divine, for, per Romans 1:18–23, God is the one who has instilled it himself. To Launonen and Mullins, proponents of the model would argue that these empirical findings have no bearing on the veracity of general revelation or whether classical theism is "natural." As Jong, Kavanagh, and Visala have argued, therefore, the yields of the cognitive science of religion may well witness instead to the human mind as a natural idolater (2015).

Second, nonetheless, the model I advance here continues to emphasize the affective, and even experiential (or existential and phenomenological) salience of the doctrine of general revelation. Given that the sense of divinity is submerged and then suppressed by sinners, Johan Bavinck argues, it manifests itself not in straightforward professions of belief in God. Rather, because humans are fallen religious creatures always in contact with God, there is an existential "unsettledness" as a result of their suppression of the sense of the divine. Furthermore, because the sense of divinity is implanted by an active work of God himself, they cannot ultimately eradicate it, and so "[the sense of divinity] cannot become openly conscious; it appears in disguise, and it is exchanged for something different" (J. Bavinck, 2023, 117–118). Indeed, as Sonderegger observes, the sense of the divine might "spring up," despite our attempts to eradicate it.

The sense of divinity pops up "in disguise" due to the heart's desire (and failure) to repress the truth. Johan Bavinck argues that the sense shows up in our intuitions and talk of norms, in our tendency to feel that there is an ultimate problem concerning the world and that there is a corresponding solution, our care for belonging, our longing for a destiny, and a connection with a higher power. However, sinners are always "exchanging" these points of reference from God to something creaturely. All of these "magnetic points" as Johan calls them, manifest the human heart's wrestling with the sense of the divine – though all humans know God, in an attempt to erase the sense of divinity, humans substitute God with another creaturely reality (J. Bavinck, 2003, 226). "General revelation is depicted for us in the bible as a much more personal involvement of God with each person than we in our theology once understood it to be. We will have to . . . disentangle them from all their abstract philosophical accretions and to understand them in terms of biblical reality" (J. Bavinck, 2003, 238). The empirical salience of the doctrine of general revelation is thus not primarily about the professions of belief that might be observed, but in the existential dimensions of human life – in its misdirected worship, fears and longings, and so on. Though sinners deny God, in other words, sinners continue to wrestle with the desires and cares that reflect their wrestling with the creator, and often fail to move this affective awareness toward accurate propositions.

To flesh this out even further, a few conceptual tools from phenomenology prove to be helpful, as we will see in the next section.

5 Can Knowledge Precede Propositions? On Phenomenology and Affective Salience

The Element has so far argued that there is a subconscious, phenomenological level of human knowing, an affective dimension to the human person, and that this is the locus of general revelation's effects. There is a kind of meaningful, human phenomenology that precedes explicit cognizing, which anticipates and addresses a potential objection concerning whether human knowledge can precede propositional awareness.[21] To flesh out Sonderegger's comments on a "phenomenological" sense of divinity and Johan Bavinck's judgments on the affective salience of general revelation, I now turn to offer a theological interpretation of Heidegger's phenomenology in light of the affective model.

5.1 A Theological Interpretation of Heidegger: Affect and Practice

Heidegger provides us with the conceptual resources to describe the meaningfulness of nonconceptual knowing and practice, such that conceptual reasoning, and even the formation of immediately formed beliefs that are "present-at-hand," do

---

[21] In the analytic literature, there is an acknowledgement of a kind of relational knowledge, or knowledge of acquaintance, or moral perception, that precedes propositionalization or concept formation. For instance, Robert Audi has argued that "moral perception may precede, and indeed may be a normal developmental route to, moral concept-formation" (2013, 46).

not get at the deepest level of human knowing. Reasoning presupposes the preconditions of *Dasein*'s contact with the world and its affordances, and takes place within the context of humanity's "cares."

Heidegger illumines this everyday phenomenology by drawing many distinctions. For our purposes, we will observe just two: between the "ontical" and the "ontological," and between that which is "ready-to-hand" and that which is "present-at-hand."

Firstly, then, for Heidegger, the *being* of *Dasein*, or rather, its "ontology," is something that is "pre-ontological," in the sense that one's existence as being precedes the *study* of being (Heidegger, 1962, 32). If "ontology" is the "theoretical inquiry" that studies being, Heidegger reasons, then one must reckon with the reality that *Dasein's* being precedes that study. *Dasein's* being, then, is "ontical," which is that which is closest, most immediate, and concrete, and hence prior to developing an ontology. The ontical refers to the concrete being of humanity. We already are human, and fully functional and inhabiting the world as human, prior to developing a *theory* of human being. This distinction between onticity and ontology produces a paradox: "Dasein is not only closest to us – even that which is closest: we *are* it, each of us, we ourselves. In spite of this, or rather for just this reason, it is ontologically that which is farthest" (Heidegger, 1962, 36; cf. Dreyfus, 1991, 21). To explicitly study human existence (ontologically) is to move ourselves away from everyday human existence (onticity), and because *Dasein* is nontheoretical, concerned, and fluid, it can only be studied indirectly: "We must rather choose such a way of access and such a kind of interpretation that this entity can show itself in itself and from itself. And this means that it is to be shown as it is *proximally and for the most part – in its average everydayness*" (Heidegger, 1962, 38; emphases original). Being precedes theoretical knowing, and thus the study of ontology removes one from concrete being, despite seeking to describe concrete being. This is not to say that the study of human ontology is unimportant (for Heidegger himself is attempting such a project), but that it is derivative, and detached from the actual concrete existence of the very being that it is supposed to study.

Secondly, that concrete existence treats the affordances of the environment in which *Dasein* finds itself as *ready-to-hand*, rather than *present-at-hand*. *Dasein* functions, in its everydayness, by rendering its environment as equipment which is ready-to-hand. Readiness-to-hand is eluded the moment we examine "the 'outward appearance' of Things in whatever form this takes," by making it present-at-hand. (Heidegger, 1962, 98). Again, "if we look at Things just 'theoretically', we can get along without understanding readiness-to-hand" (Heidegger, 1962, 98–99). However, when we deploy things in the environment, "this activity is not a blind one," and instead it has "its own kind of sight by which our manipulation is guided and from which it acquires its specific Thingly character" (Heidegger, 1962, 99). This is the context in which Heidegger introduces the example of using a hammer – the skilled carpenter uses the hammer in itself in fluid practicality, perhaps even while his mind is thinking about something else — his being, that is, his body is moving the hammer, "appropriated" it, so to speak, as that which is in-order-to (Heidegger, 1962, 98).

Only when something goes awry, say, the nail being lost, or the hammer becoming broken, does "*obtrusiveness*" occur; the object becomes present-at-hand, thus removing one's self from the very concreteness of the meaningful yet nonconceptual activity: "It reveals itself as something just-present-at-hand and no more, which cannot be budged without the thing that is missing. The helpless way in which we stand before it is a deficient mode of concern, and as such it uncovers the Being-just-present-at-hand-and-no-more of something ready-to-hand" (Heidegger, 1962, 103). The mental and present-at-hand are perhaps necessary at particular points, but the locus of meaning precedes this explicitly "thematic" way of cognition.

The insight here, for Heidegger, is that the ready-to-hand is not "founded upon" that which is "present-at-hand" (Heidegger, 1962, 101). It is not the case that meaningful being is predicated on the linguistic, propositional, or explicit, but the other way around. Predication takes place within a prior embodied sort of knowing and practicality, what Hubert Dreyfus calls "skillful coping" (Dreyfus, 2014, 116). Skillful coping contains at least these three related features: (1) conceptual reasoning and conscious acts of the will are not the primary ways in which human beings exhibit expertise. (2) Human skillfulness, instead, manifests itself in the intuitive, non- or pre-theoretical, and non-volitionally responsive ways in which one copes with environmental affordances. (3) Skillful coping does not only mark the master's expertise, but also everyday existence. Cognitive action and conceptual reflection, then, always take place in the context of "everyday practice" that lies beneath "our theoretical presuppositions and assumptions" (Dreyfus, 2014, 134).

If the structure of Heidegger's phenomenology sounds familiar to theological readers, this is because, as Judith Wolfe indicates, Heidegger was drawn to situating human reason within a prior, meaningful contact with Being-as-such because of the influence of Bonaventure's Augustinian theory of illumination: "For Bonaventure as for Heidegger, a transcendental viewpoint, which seeks the conditions of the possibility of all knowledge, does not discover a new entity, but asks after that which is no entity and yet makes possible all intentionality, and this is Being itself" (Wolfe, 2013, 117). For Bonaventure, God attends to the mind as an "unchangeable light" (Bonaventure, 2002, 3. 3.), and "it is His light that supplements or concurs with the human cognitive light so that it can truly illumine reality" (Schumacher, 2011, 142). This divine illumination is implicit or tacit, to be sure, and thus not always in the forefront of human consciousness, but the attentive human mind can discover the "divine realities that shine forth" as a result of that illumining work, disclosed in Romans 1:19–20 (Bonaventure, 2002, 2. 13). As John Webster comments: "Bonaventure is a positive divine, one for whom the mind's powers are encompassed and accompanied by a gift and light which are not of the mind's invention" (Webster, 2012, 174). Bonaventure regards divine illumination, and thus accommodated contact with the Being itself to be that which conditions and enables the possibility of reason's proper function.

If, for Bonaventure, the operation of human reason is situated within the condition of divine illumination, Heidegger demythologizes Bonaventure by asserting that this primordial contact is not with divine being, but "Being" in the sense of the imminent, affordances of the world as *Dasein*'s environment.

The affective model of the sense of divinity can remythologize Heidegger, so to speak, while accommodating his insights. God's general revelation results in the provision of intuitions that lie underneath explicit cognition or propositional awareness. The intuitions and "phenomena" of Heidegger's phenomenology are the result of everyday exposure to creation, and because God himself is the agent of revelation, and creation is a divine handiwork, one's environment is always and everywhere eliciting the "sensus divinitatis." Or, as Fritz has argued, reading Heidegger theologically would show us that "revelation, which so often is equated with the glory of transfiguration and the shining of heaven, can be found just as much in the mundane and everyday" (2021, 318).

This brings us full circle to the affective and phenomenological salience of general revelation. The sense of the divine may prompt particular instincts, propositions, or actions, which leads to a variety of religious acts or interpretations, but it remains beneath and submerged underneath them. Human beings are already always in touch with truth, and indeed, are always *in* the truth, in the sense that they are involved within "the broader phenomenon of openness to and contact with the world, and as encompassing subpropositional, propositional, and suprapropositional levels" (Inkpin, 2016, 62). Hence, as Bavinck argues, the primordial context in which humanity lives is *precisely God's self-revelation* – revelation is that which underlies all created existence. That is, in a manner more pervasive than any social or physical environment we are in, the human self is always living in the context of divine action.[22] In God, we live and

---

[22] While beyond the scope of this element, Bavinck's account of revelation presupposes the distinction between archetypal and ectypal theology and divine accommodation, and thus the

move and have our being (Acts 17:28). Since that is the case, the human self is always already skillfully coping with this primordial environment, and due to sinfulness, that skillful coping takes the form of suppression and need not be learned. God's self-revelation is the primary *affordance* that elicits our fluid coping, and it is the context out of which we reflect and make conscious decisions. Thus, read in light of Romans 1, the intuition of that environment is concurrent with the sense of divinity. This sense of divinity can prompt explicit reflection, and, as it were attended to as that which is "present-at-hand," but as Heidegger recognizes, that which becomes present-at-hand has long been known beforehand. Sin forges a disconnect between that which is present-at-hand and that which was ready-to-hand.

5.2 Three More Benefits of the Affective Model

Three further implications follow from this appropriation of Heidegger's phenomenology and the affective model of the sense of divinity, and these implications, I suggest, further highlight the model's strengths.

Firstly, as I argued in the section on the cognitive science of religion, the model highlights the affective salience of the doctrine of general revelation. The affective model accounts for why it is that humans often display a vivid tendency to ask about the meaning of their own existence as a finite creature, to seek forgiveness and atonement in the face of guilt, to contemplate a higher power or destiny when confronted with mortality or the grandeur and horrors of creation, and so on. In Heidegger's language, the affective model explains why it is that "Dasein ... is ontically distinguished by the fact that, in its very Being, that Being is an *issue* for it ... and this implies that Dasein, in its Being, has a relationship toward that Being – a relation which itself is one of Being" (Heidegger, 1962, 32; emphasis original). Humans are in touch with their existence, and relate to their existence, with profound care, and the affective model suggests that this is because, as image bearers, and due to the divine initiative, God has not left them without a witness.

Secondly, the affective model directs one's attention away from the purely epistemic or philosophical when one brings up the issue of general revelation or the noetic effects of sin, and orients it within a more concrete and affective theological anthropology. There is a tendency to conflate general revelation with the natural theological proofs of God's existence or with cognitively natural theism, or to conflate the noetic effects of sin with the inferring of wrong propositions about God, or of forming no beliefs about God at all. Those

___

pervasiveness of general revelation does not compromise the creator-creature distinction. For an account of Bavinck's broader theological epistemology, see Sutanto (2020).

issues may be philosophically interesting, but they do not get at the heart of the doctrine of general revelation, which highlights the affective dimensions of human existence. The way one experiences God in creation is not primarily, even exclusively, by way of explicit thinking, but also by way of our inhabitation, and indeed practiced immersivity in God's world (cf. Ward, 2016, 259; Hector, 2023, 2–3). The noetic effects of sin should thus be discussed alongside the affective or psychical effects of sin, according to which sinfulness is displayed in one's fluid coping and repression of the affordances of general revelation in everyday, concrete existence (See Sutanto, 2024). Unbelief and nontheism are indeed the results of the noetic and affective effects of sin: repression causes the emergence of a discrepancy between one's professions and one's affects or feelings. The space of reasons takes place within the backdrop of the phenomenological wrestling with the knowledge of God, per Sonderegger and Johan Bavinck.

Thirdly, and perhaps most importantly, the affective model of general revelation resists the domestication of Paul's and Calvin's emphases on the universality and efficacy of God's revealing work, despite the presence of unbelief and the professions of nontheists. A propositionalized or faculty-model of the sense of divinity would render the efficacy of general revelation something dependent on the presence or profession of explicit propositions in each and every person. As such, due to the noetic effects of sin and the presence of atheism, these alternative models would perhaps suggest that this propositional knowledge is either something all creatures have, or something they used to have – the noetic effects of sin thus might include a total loss of the knowledge of God.

I suggest, however, that understanding the creational knowledge of God as primarily or exclusively propositional in character risks diluting the sense of Paul's text, which denotes that human beings always suppress the knowledge of God *within the context* of *possessing* that knowledge, of having "clearly perceived" him because God himself has "shown it to them" (Rom. 1:19–20). An exclusively propositionalized model of the natural knowledge of God seems to render the efficacy of God's general revelation dependent on whether human beings do profess to believe particular propositions about God. Here, I suggest that unless one has a grasp of the possibility of an *affective* and *phenomenological* account of knowing, one would be hard-pressed to do justice to the sense of Paul's meaning. In other words, in line with Paul's witness, human beings continue to know God, even while they hold false beliefs about him, and, indeed, human beings continue to know God, even while they hold *no propositional* beliefs about God, and even when they deny God. Indeed, one of the potential weaknesses of an exclusively propositional rendering of the knowledge of God disclosed in Romans 1 is that, upon encountering nontheists, one would have to say that God's revelation is somehow not plain, or that some simply lack a knowledge of God. No amount of surveying the increase or decrease of professed atheism, however, in principle, can put to question the efficacy of general revelation, because general revelation does not have to do with propositional beliefs in the first place. Heidegger's phenomenology has shown that cognition arises out of and alongside preconscious embodied affects. If one has a phenomenological account of knowing in view, then one can hold on to the prima facie paradox that one can know God without believing any explicit propositions about God.

6 Objections: Barth, Schilder, and McFarland

This final section further clarifies some more features and benefits of the model by showing how it might address or elude the objections to the natural knowledge of God by three theologians: Karl Barth, Klaas Schilder, and Ian McFarland.

6.1 Karl Barth

Barth's rejection of natural theology, natural revelation, or the natural knowledge of God is nuanced, far-reaching, and contextually complicated, and space does not permit us to go into every detail. Here, I describe the kind of natural theology that Barth rejects, and then indicate how the affective model addresses Barth's rejection.

Though Barth declares that "even if we only lend our little finger to natural theology, there necessarily follows the denial of God in Jesus Christ," he is quite specific about what he means by natural theology (Barth, 1957, 173). After all, a "natural theology which does not strive to be the only master is not a natural theology" (Barth, 1957, 173). Barth, for instance, does not deny that nature and culture could become "instruments" of revelation, nor is the issue of natural theology so much about the indispensable role of reasoning for theological reflection. As Bruce McCormack specifies, Barth is committed to a distinction between the locus and the source or power "by means of which revelation (in the Bible or in nature and history)" becomes actualized (McCormack, 1995, 306 n. 51). The issue for Barth, as Kevin Diller specifies, is about the "latent presumption that human reason could provide neutral and independent access to the knowledge of God apart from encounter with and transformation by God" (Diller, 2015, 180). Clearly, Barth's rejection of natural theology is specific, and is targeted at a particular definition of the same. I specify three features of the natural theology he rejects.

First, Barth argues that talk of natural theology or the natural knowledge of God presumes that human reason, or some human capacity, is on its own able to arrive at some true knowledge of God, such that the knowledge of God becomes obtainable by some natural means or is rendered a property of creation itself, rather than dependent on an act of God. Natural theology assumes that God is manifested "in our creatureliness, the creation of man which is also the revelation of God" (Barth, 1936, 130). But it would be a mistake, as Barth famously argued against Emil Brunner, to suggest that some capacity in humanity could serve as a point of contact for the Word of God (Barth, 1936, 65–138). To emphasize the intrinsic ability of humanity to arrive at some natural knowledge of God would be to invite the hubris of German Nazism and the identification of its own culture as the source of knowledge of the divine will (cf. Holder, 2013, 121; Diller, 2015, 181). Revelation is thus never a property of creation in itself, nor a possession or capacity for humanity to actualize.

Furthermore, to claim that humans have an intrinsic capacity to know God risks projecting human ideas unto the divine, which presumes that God and creation are on the same plane of existence, leading to Barth's probing criticisms of the *analogia entis* as the invention of the anti-Christ (Barth, 1936, xiii; see also Johnson, 2010). Barth does not, to be clear, reject the notion of "analogy" in itself, but argues that if there is indeed some sort of correspondence between "what we say of God and what God is," it is on the basis of "the fact that God's true revelation comes from out of itself to meet what we can say with our human words and makes a selection from among them to which we have then to attach ourselves in obedience" (Barth, 1957, 227). It follows, therefore, that any "knowledge" of God is not due to the intrinsic, indeed, natural capacity of human predication or reason but is due to God's initiation and revelation, an *analogia fidei*.

Second, Barth argues that talk of natural theology involves the assumption that Christian theology must be validated by some neutral, general human standard, or involves the combination of theology from general philosophical principles and from supernatural revelation (Barth, 1957, 181). The question of the knowledge of God, however, cannot be established in the abstract but only in *the concrete*, for the word of God must be considered on its own terms. As Barth reasons:

> Just as the reality of the Word of God in Jesus Christ bears its possibility within itself, as does also the reality of the Holy Spirit, by whom the Word of God comes to man, so too the possibility of the knowledge of God and therefore the knowability of God cannot be questioned *in vacuo*, or by means of a general criterion of knowledge delimited the knowledge of God from without, but only from within this real knowledge itself. (Barth, 1957, 4)

As Diller comments, Barth was rejecting a "general starting-point assumption" typified by Enlightenment modernism, which searches for 'a shared foundation between natural and spiritual knowing' (Diller, 2015, 78; see also Green, 2013, 1–35). It is not the case that some knowledge of God is gained from general, or neutral, philosophical principles, which anticipate, verify, or are supplemented by, the material of revelation.

Third, Barth argues that revelation, properly speaking, is a revelation of the saving work of Jesus Christ. This is apparent in his exposition of Romans 1:18ff, which takes a different route than the older Reformed or Catholic readings surveyed at the beginning of this Element. Barth acknowledges that Paul is indeed talking about "man in the cosmos," and that it "is unquestionable that knowledge of God is here ascribed to man in the cosmos, and knowability is ascribed to God" (Barth, 1957, 119). However, Barth argues that we cannot read Paul here as if he was some "unknown secular author," and thus his words must be seen in light of the gospel in Rom. 1:17 (Barth, 1957, 119). Paul is not "speaking of the heathen in themselves and in general," but rather about "the revelation of the grace of God in Jesus Christ" (Barth, 1957, 119). This revelation of the gospel always has a "shadow side," namely, "the wrath of God," and "it is of this shadow side that he speaks in the first part of the epistle" (Barth, 1957, 119). Barth is therefore rejecting any clear distinction between general and special revelation, and that revelation, if it is truly a revelation, must be redemptive and thus be about and from the grace of Jesus Christ (cf. Diller, 2015, 192; Duby, 2019, 123).[23]

How does the affective model address Barth's objections? To the first objection, it is worth noting that the affective model does not locate the revelation of God as a property of creation itself, to be mined or domesticated by some intrinsic human capacity. Nor does the affective model suggest that the "point of contact" just is the structure of human nature, which manifests the being of God in some way. Rather, the "point of contact" is due solely to the divine initiative, by means of creation, which implants a feeling of the divine in each human heart. It is not the case, then, that human reason is baptized or mandated to produce some true knowledge of God, on its own, which then anticipates supernatural theology, for the sense of divinity is not, technically speaking, about human reason at all. This is why, as we have seen, Bavinck was uncomfortable with the terminology of "natural theology" and insisted that "according to Scripture, all revelation, also that in nature, is supernatural" (H. Bavinck,

---

[23] See also the exploration of Barth's discussion of the "little lights of creation" in *Church Dogmatics* IV/3 and whether Barth re-introduced natural theology through Christology in Fergusson (2016). For earlier explorations of Barth and natural theology, see Torrance (1990), Rogers (1999), and Hunsinger (2015).

2003, 307). The affective model evades Barth's objection here because it insists that the bestowal of the feeling of the divine is a divine act, due to a sovereign initiative of divine freedom.

The response to the second objection follows from the first. Because the sense of the divine is a repressed feeling in the subconscious, it cannot serve as a starting point for a positive, Christian, theological construction. It serves as a "point of contact" only in the sense that the redemptive word in Christ addresses the existential striving of the human heart that has been stirred by that feeling of divinity. Bavinck himself, as early as 1904, was critical of the emerging German nationalism that began to identify German culture with the locus of divine revelation (see Sutanto, 2024, chs. 6–7). The affective model could well accommodate and even agree with Barth's insistence that Christian theology is grounded in revelation alone, and does not consist in a combination of a generic, philosophical theology of "pure nature" alongside the illumination of the faith. Indeed, Bavinck saw himself as standing on the Reformational recovery of the intrinsic "bond between special and general revelation" (Bavinck, 2003, 305). He suggested that the Reformed were responding to what he perceived to be a dualistic structure in Roman Catholic prolegomena, according to which "knowing and believing, reason and authority, natural and supernatural revelation, occur dualistically side by side" (Bavinck, 2003, 304). As such, the "Reformation took over this distinction between natural and supernatural revelation while nevertheless in principle assigning a very different meaning to it," for they insisted that Scripture and illumination are necessary for humans to interpret general revelation properly (Bavinck, 2003, 304). In the language of the affective model, special revelation and the illumination of the Spirit are required for us to see clearly that we have been wrestling with the feelings of guilt and dependence instilled by the sense of the divine.

The response to the third objection is admittedly a bit less straightforward. While the affective model of Johan and Herman Bavinck would agree against sharpening a distinction between general and special revelation, the model would continue to preserve that there is, indeed, a distinction between them – God discloses himself by two means: general revelation is affective while special revelation includes verbal and propositional means. General revelation, again, is repressed by the sinful human condition, and is not to be taken on its own as a prompt for a generic, pre-dogmatic natural theological program. This, it seems, is more in keeping with the sense of Romans 1:18–32, and the traditioned interpretation of the same. Steven Duby registers a similar response towards Barth, drawing from Thomas Aquinas:

> Before and after this section, Paul uses second-person pronouns and verbs to address his readership (Rom. 1:15, 21), but here he is speaking broadly in the third person about 'humans who suppress the truth'. Such persons already know of God's eternal power and deity and of their own wrong-doing – and they know these things by the created order ... with no indication that this knowledge is given only in an evangelistic explanation of creation and human guilt. This is why such persons are culpable before God, and that is why the proclamation of the gospel is so urgent. To take a up a distinction noted ... from Thomas, humanity's ignorance of God in Romans 1 is not theoretical but 'affective', meaning that they do not know God in that they do not love and worship him as they ought. In this connection, natural knowledge of God is not, as Barth worried, a means of human self-justification before God but rather the exact opposite: an awareness that none of us is righteous before God, even if that awareness might be temporarily pushed aside. (Duby, 2019, 121)

General revelation, as Paul indicates and as Duby discerns, organically anticipates the message of redemption only as guilt corresponds to grace. The affective model would further emphasize that the sinner knows these things by the created order precisely because the created order is an instrument in *God's* hands, and it is God who discloses himself through them, rather than us who discover God through creation.

When the sinner is captivated by the redeeming and sanctifying work of the Spirit, the renewed intellect can indeed see in creation the glimmers of the glory of God, with special revelation providing the criteria and principles for such work, and this is what distinguishes the *theologia vera* from *theologia falsa* (Turretin, 1992, 1. 2. 5). The affective model's insistence that the sense of divinity is not reducible to a set of propositions, nor of philosophical reasoning, has the double benefit of evading Barth's first two concerns, emphasizing that revelation is a divine work that does not affirm the positive deployment of unregenerate reason for constructing dogmatics, while simultaneously maintaining a continuity with the older traditioned readings of Romans 1 on the distinction between general and special revelation.

The response to Barth here provides the groundwork for my responses to Schilder and McFarland.

6.2 Klaas Schilder

Klaas Schilder was a Dutch Reformed theologian who worked in the neo-Calvinist tradition of Kuyper and Bavinck, and, like Barth, registered a firm "no" to "general revelation and natural theology" (Schilder, 2022, 178). Schilder does not make a strong distinction between general revelation and natural theology, and he focuses his critique in his 1939 commentary on the Heidelberg Catechism. Like Barth, however, he is focusing his critique on a rather specific definition of general revelation and its effects. He does not deny, for instance, that there is a "natural knowledge of God" that can be gained by Christians "*at the hand of Scripture*" (Schilder, 2022, 183). Rather, he has in view the conflation of revelation with some feature of the human condition, and, more specifically, with the work of the human conscience through a misuse or misinterpretation of Romans 2:14–15.

Schilder's objections can be boiled down to two interconnected reasons: he suggests that the doctrine of general revelation leads to a speculative identification of human-made principles with revelation, and subsequently, therefore, to an unduly positive and elevated view of the unbelieving mind and heart. Because these two reasons are so intertwined, I shall treat them together.

Schilder observes the history of Reformed interpretations of Romans 2:14–15 and argues that they wrongly affirmed that "an extensive knowledge was available to the conscience of natural man, even apart from Scripture" (Schilder, 2022, 184). This might take the form of identifying the Stoic idea of "common notions" with general revelation, which provided principles "in the field of ethics," or in the identification of axioms with "natural law," such that these principles and axioms became normative alongside the word of God (Schilder, 2022, 189–190). To exacerbate matters, Schilder observes that this leads to the identification of the institutions and cultures built on the basis of these purportedly revealed axioms with the results of revelation itself, and this leads to a dangerous, chauvinistic sort of hubris. In Schilder's mind, just as it would be foolish to identify "the time and morals in a certain age" of the Christian church in, say, "the Middle ages" with *the* work of special revelation, so would it be foolish "if you were to depict the life of the *heathens* just by saying 'Behold, the work of *general* revelation!'" (Schilder, 2022, 201; emphases original). At every point, Schilder argues, one should be mindful of the distinction between revelation itself, and how "people *react* and *respond* to it" (Schilder, 2022, 200; emphases original).

This identification of revelation with human principles and axioms is, in Schilder's judgment, what led past theologians to misuse Rom. 2:14–5 in order to pronounce a "Magnificat" to humanity in general, and to how "things are 'not all that bad' in my case" (Schilder, 2022, 199). His concern is the move of excusing or rendering positive judgments on the unbeliever due to their possession of general revelation, as if the "situation in which they find themselves is therefore not all that bad" (Schilder, 2022, 197). By contrast, Schilder argues that Romans 1–2 does not affirm a light in unregenerate humanity, as some kind of intrinsically praiseworthy human capacity. Rather, the point in these passages is that the sinful nature is culpable and corrupt, leaving them without excuse. The conscience and the "light" are not an affirmation of humanity but a witness to culpability. As such, Schilder argues that the conscience should not be considered as itself revealing God. Referring to Psalm 19, Schilder writes that "you *cannot* just consider conscience a part of general revelation, and simply apply to it what Scripture reports – in a poem, no less! – about the heavens, which declare the glory of God, and about the sky, which proclaims his handiwork" (Schilder, 2022, 207; emphasis original). Schilder hardens the distinction already found in earlier neo-Calvinists between revelation from creation and human reasoning – excluding as well the work of the fallen conscience as revelatory of God. Though Schilder affirms that "remnants" of the image of God remain in fallen humanity, he warns against using this language as an affirmation of the human being: "Will someone now turn to sing the praises of that natural light? Or the praises of the remnants? Or the praises of the conscience? Let them rather sing the praises of *God*, who preserves the 'nature' of his creatures, regardless of how fiercely they struggle against it" (Schilder, 2022, 209). Schilder concludes that the point of Romans 2:14–15, along with 1:18–23, is not the elevation of sinful human knowing as still trustworthy or praiseworthy, but as disclosing guilt and culpability.

By way of response, it is important to note that despite the polemical tone of Schilder's objections, he never denies that there is a proper recognition of "some light of nature" in fallen humanity, but that light is "corrupted, suppressed, and resisted because of the flesh" (Schilder, 2022, 209). I suggest that the affective model preserves Schilder's affirmation of this light of nature, and can also alleviate his worries about whether this affirmation would lead to the identification of the principles of human reason with revelation, or to a positive affirmation of the fallen mind. Indeed, to repeat the point towards Barth, the affective model can do this because the result of general revelation is *not propositional* and is not about the product of human reason at all.

By identifying the effect of general revelation with the sensus numinis, one can distinguish between revelation's effects and the conceptual reception of that revelation by the human intellect. It is thus inappropriate simply to identify the notions of the Stoics with general revelation or the principles of some culture with the dictates of natural law, especially apart from the illumination of the word and Spirit. The senus numinis may *stir* the human mind to produce such principles, but those principles may be diverse, are not themselves revelation, and must be evaluated by special revelation. Thus, no single culture or institution can be identified intrinsically with possessing a deposit of revelation that naturally anticipates or is seamlessly compossible with special revelation. In these ways, the model can accommodate Schilder's worries and avoid the pitfalls that he identifies.

The model, however, also preserves the classical teaching that the created mind, when illumined by the Spirit, may indeed positively and explicitly reflect on those affects. Schilder himself does this as he considers the implications of the suppression of the light of nature, and Paul, too, identifies in propositional language what those affects *signify* in Rom. 1:18–23, 32. However, because those affects precede conceptual reasoning, any form of human conceptual reasoning is never identical with revelation but is either consistent with, obedient to, or inconsistent with that revelation. The affective model, therefore *relativizes* human reasoning, and resists the identification of one particular human culture with revelation, precisely because it emphasizes that revelation is solely a divine activity, with a locus of reception that precedes propositional knowing. Scripture, illumination, and the Spirit norm the human interpretation and reception of general revelation and renders possible the conformity of reason to revelation. For emphasis, the affective model, in other words, eludes Schilder's worries while preserving his insight that one should always mind the gap between revelation and human reception and interpretation. I also suggest that, far from affirming the consciousness or conscience of fallen humanity, the model highlights the patience and mercy of God, who continues to disclose himself to all people, despite their repression and misuse of that sense.

6.3 Ian McFarland

Finally, then, I suggest that the affective model and its phenomenological emphases prove fruitful as it addresses the more recent dogmatic work of Ian McFarland against the natural knowledge of God (McFarland, 2014; 2016). McFarland focuses on the epistemological implications of his understanding of divine transcendence and God's exhaustive involvement within the world. In so doing, he articulates a potent and theologically motivated rejection of the natural knowledge of God, not because, as some might predict, of the positing of God's hiddenness or inactivity within the world but precisely because of God's immanence. Put positively, "a maximally comprehensive vision of divine involvement in the world," he writes, actually makes "untenable any direct line of inference from creature to Creator, in the form of claims that the beauty or order of the world reveal God" (McFarland, 2016, 260). Precisely because God is comprehensively involved in the world, there is no direct epistemic access to God in one place or another. McFarland's line of argumentation climaxes in this arresting passage:

> Since all creatures are equally and absolutely dependent on God for every
> aspect of their existence and at every point of their existence, no aspect of

created reality can in itself provide any privileged line of access to the divine. Nor can the structure of the created order as a whole serve this purpose. Because God transcends all creatures, whether considered individually or as a collective, to the same infinite degree, one can no more ascend to God via the experience of any particular set of natural phenomena than Esther Summerson might infer the existence of Charles Dickens based on her experience of the novelistic world of *Bleak House*. The connection between god and the world, like that between the author and his novel, is visible only to one who has a view of both – and that is something we do not have – except insofar as God provides that perspective by revealing God's self within creation. Otherwise, creation remains opaque to God, not because God is distant from it, but precisely because God's all-encompassing relation to the world as 'the Father almighty' precludes the creature acquiring any point of epistemic leverage over against the Creator. (McFarland, 2016, 270–271)

McFarland's claims here concerning the implications of the opaqueness of creation and the inability of human reasoning to infer theological claims in a bottom-up fashion are complemented in the following passage from his *From Nothing*:

Creation from nothing implies that god is *already* maximally "inside" the world: since God's sustaining presence is the one necessary and sufficient condition of every creature's existence at every moment of its existence, any degree of divine absence would result in the total and instantaneous dissolution of created being (see Ps. 104:29) . . . Creation from nothing rules out talk of any creature existing apart from or at any distance from God. It follows that God is and cannot be *more* present in Jesus than in you or me or the lowliest sea slug. (McFarland, 2014, 102)

The creator-creature distinction means that from one creaturely phenomenon only another creaturely phenomenon can be inferred, and the doctrine of God's omnipresence and his exhaustive involvement with the world means that no particular aspect of creation provides a privileged entryway toward knowledge of God. Just as characters within a novel could never infer the existence or character of the author from the features internal to the causal nexus of the novel, so creatures cannot reason unto God from creational phenomena for "in so doing we are tracing a connection between one phenomenon and another – here to there, now to then, this to that. But if God is not one object among others, then there can be no reasoning from phenomenal entities to God" (McFarland, 2022, 69). The invisibility of God is the entailment of the relation between creator and creature.

Theological reasoning with respect to creation and the being of God, therefore, belongs within the standpoint of a confessing faith rather than a set of deduced claims from empirical observation or by virtue of sheer logical acumen. McFarland's suspicions concerning the epistemic success of natural theological reasoning are thus similar to Bavinck's (and neo-Calvinism's) dispositions: both emphasize the necessity of starting with the Christian faith for proper dogmatic reflection, and hence both would render suspect a pre-dogmatic model of natural theology. Neo-Calvinist dogmaticians would similarly emphasize the transcendence of God and God's exhaustive preservation and governance of the world by way of concursus.

McFarland's exegetical emphasis on Romans 1, too, would be shared by the neo-Calvinist: whatever knowledge or talk of God that arises in the creature's experience of the world renders that creature's thinking "futile" because "they invariably confuse God with some lesser reality . . . with more abstract forms of first cause, unmoved mover, or most perfect being in what remains a worldly matrix of cause and effect" (McFarland, 2016, 272). As we saw, Abraham Kuyper had argued very similarly that from "the finite no conclusion can be drawn to the infinite, neither can a Divine reality be known from external or internal phenomena, unless that real God *reveals* Himself in my consciousness to my ego" (Kuyper, 1898, 343). The emphasis in Romans 1 is thus not the possibility of a "perception of the invisible with a movement from phenomenal effect to transcendent cause," which would be to commit a "category error," but about the "One who comes to be known in questioning *us*" (McFarland, 2016, 273). The direction must come from the top-down as the God of Jesus Christ, who is recognized by those who are "in faith" (McFarland, 2016, 273).

Yet, as we've seen, the affective model affirms the ubiquity of general revelation whereas McFarland deemed it fitting to deny it as a useful category altogether (McFarland, 2016, 261, n. 3). At least one reason this is the case, given the affective model (and phenomenological account) of general revelation, is that the natural knowledge of God is not primarily a rational category but an affective one. Creation reveals and bestows a knowledge of God that is not the product of reasoning from created effects toward a transcendent cause, but a pressure exerted by a ubiquitous divine revelation that incurs a phenomenological, relational awareness of the creature's failure to honor its creator. Much like how the awareness that a spouse is angry arises when one enters into a room merely by recognizing the spouse's body language – without the attendance of words – God's pervasive presence means, in dogmatic terms, that no creature exists without their awareness of their failures and dependence before their creator. Further, the unillumined reflection on divine realities that may be prompted by the sensus divinitatis, proponents of this model would insist, do remain futile, as they invariably confuse God with a lesser reality, refusing to acknowledge the God who is, due to sinful repression. Talk of God is to be distinguished from general revelation as a verbalized second moment, thereby preserving on the one hand the pervasiveness and efficacy of general revelation alongside the futility of reasoning unto God apart from faith. Those in Christ can, and do, behold the presence of God in creation, but this is only due to the illumination of the word and Spirit, and in a manner that preserves the analogical mode of theological predication. In these ways, it seems to me that the affective model of general revelation addresses McFarland in a similar way as it addresses the worries of Barth and Schilder. The model can assuage McFarland's worries without paying the price of denying the traditioned category altogether.

7 Conclusion

This Element has advanced an affective model of general revelation, which draws from the writings of the neo-Calvinist tradition (especially in Herman and Johan Bavinck) and a theological interpretation of the phenomenology of Martin Heidegger. I have argued that the affective model addresses the questions introduced at the beginning of this work: that the sense of the divine refers to an implanted feeling of dependence in every person, that it does better justice to the biblical and Christian witnesses to the universality of the knowledge of God than a faculty-model, that it offers a theological reorientation of the findings of the cognitive science of religion, that it locates the affective salience of the doctrine of general revelation in the phenomenological cares (or so-called magnetic points) that perennially draws the attention of agents, and that it addresses the influential objections of recent theology against the doctrine.

I began by surveying the biblical and traditioned witnesses on general revelation and the "natural knowledge of God," indicating that, though there exists a diversity of emphases throughout the history of the doctrine, there is a minimal account of this doctrine, according to which God has sufficiently disclosed himself, through creation, as the creator and judge to every creature, thus leaving them without excuse in their failure to acknowledge God. I then turned to the presentation of the model, which argues that the effect of general revelation precedes the formation of propositions, in a sensus numinis (Johan Bavinck), or a feeling of divinity, resulting in a feeling of dependence (Herman Bavinck). After distinguishing this affective model from Plantinga's "faculty-model," I then turned to show how the model theologically reorients the findings of the cognitive science of religion, showing that it is a benefit of the model to resist identifying the propositions of cognitively natural theism with the output of general revelation, and that the affective salience of the sense of the divine lies mainly in the implicit phenomenological cares sinners continue to have as a result of their unsuccessful suppression of the sense. I flesh out the phenomenological dimensions of the affective model by theologically reinterpreting some concepts from Martin Heidegger, arguing that human reasoning takes place within the context of fluid coping and exposure to divine revelation. I then highlighted three more benefits to the model: its affective salience, its interfacing with a deeper theological anthropology, and its ability to do justice to the efficacy and universality of general revelation even while acknowledging the presence of nontheism. Finally, I then turned to the objections of Karl Barth, Klaas Schilder, and Ian McFarland against the natural knowledge of God, and further clarified the strengths of the model by showing how it might address their important concerns. This Element has thus shown that the affective model is a more theologically satisfying account of general revelation and vindicates the doctrine by showing its explanatory powers and how it might address contemporary concerns.

Where do we go from here? In closing, I highlight three further possible implications of this Element for future investigation. Firstly, it should be emphasized that a postmortem evaluation of the doctrine of general revelation cannot be sustained. This Element's advancement of the affective model shows that an affective reorienting of the doctrine of general revelation and its impact on the human psyche may be key in rehabilitating this important doctrine from its twentieth-century detractors, without taking away their proper concerns. Moreover, by showing that there are multiple models of general revelation on offer, it is uncovered that these influential objections do not have the doctrine *per se* in view, but only with a particular *model* – one that suggests that general revelation allows for some neutral or rational starting point to infer right things about God, even for the unillumined mind.

Secondly, the affective model shows that an affirmation of the natural knowledge of God does not depend on the availability of an empirically verifiable universal consensus or uniformity of theistic beliefs across the globe, and is, I suggest, compatible with what we know about the diversity of religious beliefs. The natural awareness of God is indeed universal, but the *articulation* or *profession* of that knowledge may well radically differ from person to person, and from culture to culture. This is because there is always a firm distinction between the phenomenological impact of general revelation and its propositionalized articulation, the latter of which is contingent on whether the human agent is suppressing or accepting the deep-seated sense of the divine. Given the discussion of the magnetic points and the Pauline teachings that humans will substitute the glory of God for creaturely realities, each person might identify their ultimate trust (for a higher power, belonging, destiny, and so on) in differing entities. To say it another way, the affective model shows that the plurality of religious (or nonreligious) professions of beliefs serves only to *confirm* that everyone is already wrestling with the natural awareness of God, which explains why it is that humans continue to be drawn to these magnetic points. God does not leave himself without a witness (Acts 14:17).

Finally, this model reorients discussions on the noetic effects of sin and refocuses the Christian witness on the gospel. The noetic effects of sin are often discussed in a primarily philosophical mode, concerning the false propositions or erroneous inferences one makes with respect to the theistic beliefs produced by our cognitive faculties. However, the affective model suggests that nonbelief is not primarily an intellectual but an affective problem. Failure to acknowledge God is not due to the lack of arguments, evidence, or awareness of the knowledge of God but due to the corruption of sin. Sinful humanity does not want God to exist, for acknowledging God's existence and glory means simultaneously acknowledging its maximal vulnerability before him (Rom. 1:32). Hence, Christian witness involves unmasking that the root of nonbelief is not ignorance but culpable suppression. If the genesis of failure to believe in God is affective as much as it may be intellectual, as sinners are incentivized to resist God due to our vulnerability in culpability, then the Christian witness must be presented with and shaped by the gospel from the outset. Exposure of culpability is painful and heart-wrenching, and only the gospel of grace can salve the fear that keeps one from freely confessing one's guilt or shame before God. A Christian witness should keep in view that the same truth that exposes sinners is also a proclamation of a grace that offers forgiveness and reconciliation (Jn. 1:17).

References

Adams, E. (2001). Calvin's View of Natural Knowledge of God. *International Journal of Systematic Theology*, 3, 280–92.

Audi, R. (2013). *Moral Perception*. Princeton: Princeton University Press.

Augustine. (1993). *City of God*. Translated by Marcus Dods. New York: Modern Library.

Augustine. (2012). *The Trinity*. Translated by E. Hill. Hyde Park: New City Press.

Aquinas, T. (1968). *Summa Theologiae*. Translated by M. Browne. London: Eyre & Spottiswoode.

Aquinas, T. (1980) *Commentary on the Gospel of John*. Translated by J. A. Weisheipl and F. R. Larcher. Albany: Magi.

Barrett, J. (2004). *Why Would Anyone Believe in God?* Walnut Creek: Altamitra Press.

Barrett, J. (2021). Revelation and Cognitive Science: An Invitation. In B. M. Mezei, F. A. Murphy, and K. Oakes, eds., *The Oxford Handbook of Divine Revelation*. Oxford: Oxford University Press, 518–36.

Barth. K. (1934). No! Answer to Emil Brunner. In J. Bailie, ed. *Natural Theology*. Translated by P. Fraenkel. London: Centenary Press, 65–128.

Barth, K. (1936). *The Doctrine of the Word of God*. Vol I of *Church Dogmatics*. 2nd ed. Translated by G. W. Bromiley. G. W. Bromiley and T. F. Torrance, eds. Edinburgh: T&T Clark.

Barth, K. (1957). *The Doctrine of God*. Vol II of *Church Dogmatics*. Translated by T. H. L. Parker, W. B. Johnston, Harold Knight, J. L. M. Haire. G. W. Bromiley and T. F. Torrance, eds. Edinburgh: T&T Clark.

Basil. (2011). *Against Eunomius*. Translated by M. DelCogliana and A. R. Gallwitz. Washington, DC: Catholic University of America Press.

Bavinck, H. (1892). Hoofd en Hart. *Christophilus: Jaarboekje Nederlandsch Jongelings-Verbond*, 71–75.

Bavinck, H. (1897). *Beginselen der Psychologie*. Kampen: Bos.

Bavinck, H. (1909a). *Magnalia Dei: Onderwijzing in de christelijke religie naar gereformeerde belijdenis*. Kampen: Kok.

Bavinck, H. (1909b). Calvin and Common Grace. In W. P. Armstrong, ed. *Calvin and the Reformation*. Translated by G. Vos. New York: Fleming H. Revell, 99–130.

Bavinck, H. (2003). *Prolegomena*. Vol. I of *Reformed Dogmatics*. Translated by J. Vriend. J. Bolt, ed. Grand Rapids: Baker Academic.

Bavinck, H. (2004). *God and Creation*. Vol. 2 of *Reformed Dogmatics*. Translated by J. Vriend. J. Bolt, ed. Grand Rapids: Baker Academic.

Bavinck, H. (2008). *Essays on Religion, Science, and Society*. Translated by H. Boonstra and G. Sheeres. J. Bolt, ed. Grand Rapids: Baker Academic.

Bavinck, H. (2018a). Foundations of Psychology. Translated by J. V. Born, N. Kloosterman, and J. Bolt. *The Bavinck Review*, 9, 1–270.

Bavinck, H. (2018b). *Philosophy of Revelation: A New Edition*. C. Brock and N. G. Sutanto, eds. Peabody: Hendrickson.

Bavinck, H. (2019). *Christian Worldview*. Translated and edited by N. G. Sutanto, J. Eglinton, and C. C. Brock. Wheaton: Crossway.

Bavinck, H. (2021). Head and Heart. Translated by G. Parker Jr. *Modern Reformation*. https://modernreformation.org/resource-library/articles/head-and-heart/ (accessed November 10, 2021).

Bavinck, H. (2022). *Guidebook on the Instruction of the Christian Religion*. Translated by G. Parker Jr. and C. Clausing. Peabody: Hendricksen.

Bavinck, J. (1940). Het problem der anknüpfung bij Evangelieverkondiging. *Vox Theologica*, 11, 105–111.

Bavinck, J. (1941). *Het problem van de pseudo-religie en de algemeene openbaring*. Reunisten Organisatie.

Bavinck, J. (2013). *The J.H. Bavinck Reader*. Translated by J. A. De Jong. J. Bolt, J. Bratt, and P. J. Visser, eds. Grand Rapids: Eerdmans.

Bavinck, J. (2023). *The Church Between Temple and Mosque: A Study of the Relationship between Chrristianity and the Other Religions*. Glenside: Westminster Seminary Press.

Bonaventure. (1979). *Disputed Questions on the Mystery of the Trinity*. Translated by Z. Hayes. G. Marcil, ed. St. Bonaventure: The Franciscan Institute.

Bonaventure. (2002). *Itinerarium Mentis in Deum*. Translated by Z. Hayes. P. Boehner and Z Hayes, eds. St. Bonaventure: The Franciscan Institute.

Bratt, J. D. (2013). *Abraham Kuyper: Modern Calvinist, Christian Democrat*. Grand Rapids: Eerdmans.

Brock, C. (2020). *Orthodox yet Modern: Herman Bavinck's Use of Schleiermacher*. Bellingham: Lexham Press.

Calvin, J. (1961). *Institutes of the Christian Religion*. Translated by F. L. Battles. J. McNeill, ed. Library of Christian Classics. London: SCM.

Case, B. (2021). Bonaventure's Critique of Thomas Aquinas. churchlifejournal. nd.edu/articles/bonaventures-critique-of-thomas-aquinas/.

Clark, K. J. (2019). *God and the Brain: The Rationality of Religious Belief*. Grand Rapids: Eerdmans.

Clark, K. J., and Barrett, J. (2011). Reidian Religious Epistemology and the Cognitive Science of Religion. *Journal of the American Academy of Religion*, 79, 639–675.

Copleston, F. (1950). *Medieval Philosophy*. Vol. 2 of *A History of Western Philosophy*. New York: Doubleday.

Cullen, C. (2006). *Bonaventure*. Oxford: Oxford University Press.

Dennett, D. (2006). *Breaking the Spell: Religion as a Natural Phenomenon*. New York: Penguin Books.

Diller, K. (2015). *Theology's Epistemological Dilemma: How Karl Barth and Alvin Plantinga Offer a Unified Response*. Downers Grove: IVP Academic.

Dowey, E. (1994). *The Knowledge of God in Calvin's Theology*. 3rd ed. Grand Rapids: Eerdmans.

Dreyfus, H. (1991). *Being-in-the-World: A Commentary on Heidegger's* Being and Time, *Division I*. Cambridge, MA: MIT Press.

Dreyfus, H. (2014). Overcoming the Myth of the Mental: How Philosophers Can Benefit from the Phenomenology of Everyday Expertise. In M. Wrathall, ed., *Skillful Coping: Essays on the Phenomenology of Everyday Perception and Action*. Oxford: Oxford University Press, 104–124.

Duby, S. (2019). *God in Himself: Scripture, Metaphysics, and the Task of Christian Theology*. Downers Grove: IVP Academic.

Eglinton, J. (2012). *Trinity and Organism: Toward a New Reading of Herman Bavinck's Organic Motif*. London: T&T Clark.

Fergusson, D. (2016). Karl Barth's Doctrine of Creation: Church-bells Beyond the Stars. *International Journal of Systematic Theology*, 18, 414–431.

Fritz, J. P. (2021). Revelation in Heidegger. In B. M. Mezei, F. A. Murphy, and K. Oakes, eds., *The Oxford Handbook of Divine Revelation*. Oxford: Oxford University Press, 309–321.

Green, G. (2013). Barth as Theorist of Religion. In J. H. Brooke, R. R. Manning, and F. Watts, eds., *Karl Barth On Religion*. Translated by G. Green. London: Bloomsbury, 1–35.

Hector, K. (2015). *The Theological Project of Modernism: Faith and the Conditions of Mineness*. Oxford: Oxford University Press.

Hector, K. (2023). *Christianity as a Way of Life: A Systematic Theology*. New Haven: Yale University Press.

Heidegger, M. (1962). *Being and Time*. Translated by J. Macquarrie and E. Robinson. Oxford: Blackwell.

Holder, R. D. (2013). Natural Theology in the Twentieth-Century. In J. H. Brooke, R. R. Manning, and F. Watts, eds., *The Oxford Handbook of Natural Theology*. Oxford: Oxford University Press, 118–135.

Hunsinger, G. (2015). The "Yes" in Barth's "No" to Brunner: The First Commandment as a Theological Axiom. In *Evangelical, Reformed, and Catholic: Doctrinal Essays on Barth and Related Themes*. Grand Rapids: Eerdmans, 85–105.

Inkpin, A. (2016). *Disclosing the World: On the Phenomenology of Language*. Cambridge, MA: MIT Press.

Johnson, K. (2010). *Karl Barth and the Analogia Entis*. London: T&T Clark.

Jong, J., Kavanaugh, C., & Visala, A. (2015). Born Idolators: The Limits of the Philosophical Implications of the Cognitive Science of Religion. *Neue Zeitschrift für Systematische Theologie und Religionsphilosophie*, 57, 244–266.

Junius, F. (2014). *A Treatise on True Theology*. Translated by D. Noe. Grand Rapids: Reformation Heritage.

Kuyper, A. (1898). *Encyclopaedia of Sacred Theology*. Translated by H. de Vries. New York: Charles Scribner's Sons.

Kuyper, A. (2015). The Natural Knowledge of God. Translated by H. van Dyke. *The Bavinck Review*, 6, 73–112.

Launonen, L., and Mullins, R. T. (2021). Why Open Theism is Natural and Classical Theism is Not. *Religions*, 12, 1–16.

MacDonald, S. (2017). Augustine. In W. Abraham and F. Aquino, eds., *The Oxford Handbook of the Epistemology of Theology*. Oxford: Oxford University Press, 354–368.

Manning, R. R. (2013). Protestant Perspective on Natural Theology. In J. H. Brooke, R. R. Manning, and F. Watts, eds., *The Oxford Handbook of Natural Theology*. Oxford: Oxford University Press, 197–212.

Marrone, S. (2001). *The Light of Thy Countenance: Science and the Knowledge of God in the Thirteenth Century*. Vol 1 of *A Doctrine of Divine Illumination*. Leiden: Brill.

McAllister, B., and Dougherty, T. (2019). Reforming Reformed Epistemology: A New Take on the *Sensus Divinitatis*. *Religious Studies*, 55, 537–57.

McCormack, B. (1995). *Karl Barth's Critically Realistic Dialectical Theology: It's Genesis and Development, 1909–1936*. Oxford: Clarendon Press.

McFarland, I. (2014). *From Nothing: A Theology of Creation*. Louisville: Westminster John Knox.

McFarland, I. (2016). "God, the Father Almighty": A Theological Excursus. *International Journal of Systematic Theology*, 18, 259–73.

McFarland, I. (2022). Rethinking Nature and Grace: The Logic of Creation's Consummation. *International Journal of Systematic Theology*, 24, 56–79.

McFarland, I. (2024). *From Nothing: A Theology of Creation*. Louisville: Westminster John Knox.

McNabb, T. (2018). *Religious Epistemology.* Cambridge: Cambridge University Press.

Muller, R. (2000). *The Unaccommodated Calvin: Studies in the Foundation of a Theological Tradition.* Oxford: Oxford University Press.

Muller, R. (2003). *Post-Reformation Reformed Dogmatics.* Four Volumes. Grand Rapids: Baker Academic.

Plantinga, A. (2000). *Warranted Christian Belief.* Oxford: Oxford University Press.

Plantinga, A. (2015). *Knowledge and Christian Belief.* Grand Rapids: Eerdmans.

Rogers, E. (1999). *Thomas Aquinas and Karl Barth: Sacred Doctrine and the Natural Knowledge of God.* Notre Dame: University of Notre Dame Press.

Schaefer, D. O. (2015). *Religious Affects: Animality, Evolution, and Power.* Durham: Duke University Press.

Schilder, K. (2022). *The Klaas Schilder Reader.* G. Harinck, R. Mouw, and M. De Jong, eds. Bellingham: Lexham Press.

Schleiermacher, F. (2016). *Christian Faith: A New Translation and Critical Edition.* Translated by C. L. Kelsey, E. Lawler, T. N. Tice, C. L. Kelsey, T. N. Tice, eds., Louisville: Westminster John Knox.

Schumacher, L. (2011). *Divine Illumination: The History and Future of Augustine's Theory of Knowledge.* Oxford: Wiley & Blackwell.

Sonderegger, K. (2021). The Doctrine of God. In M. Allen and S. R. Swain, eds., *The Oxford Handbook of Reformed Theology.* Oxford: Oxford University Press, 389–403.

Steinmetz, D. (1995). *Calvin in Context.* Oxford: Oxford University Press.

Streetman. R. (1986). Romanticism and the Sensus Numinis in Schleiermacher. In D. Jasper, ed., *The Interpretation of Belief: Coleridge, Schleiermacher and Romanticism.* London: Palgrave McMillan, 104–125.

Sudduth, M. (2009). *The Reformed Objection to Natural Theology.* New York: Routledge.

Sutanto, N. G. (2018). Herman Bavinck and Thomas Reid on Perception and Knowing God. *Harvard Theological Review*, 111, 115–134.

Sutanto, N. G. (2020). *God and Knowledge: Herman Bavinck's Theological Epistemology.* London: Bloomsbury T&T Clark.

Sutanto, N. G. (2024) *God and Humanity: Herman Bavinck and Theological Anthropology.* London: Bloomsbury T&T Clark.

Thysius, A., Polyander, J., Rivetus, A., & Walaeus, A. (2014). *Disputations 1–23.* Vol. I of *Synopsis Purioris Theologiae: Latin Text and English Translation.* Translated by D. te Velde and R. A. Faber. D. te Veldete Velde, ed. Leiden: Brill.

Torrance, T. F. (1990). Natural Theology in the Thought of Karl Barth. In *Karl Barth, Biblical and Evangelical Theologian*. Edinburgh: T&T Clark, 136–159.

Turretin, F. (1992). *First through Tenth Topics*. Vol. 1 of *Institutes of Elenctic Theology*. Translated by G. M. Giger. J. T. Dennison Jr., ed. Phillipsburg: P&R.

Van den Brink, G. (2020). *Reformed Theology and Evolutionary Theory*. Grand Rapids: Eerdmans.

Van der Kooi, C. (2005). *As in a Mirror: John Calvin and Karl Barth on Knowing God*. Translated by D. Mader. Leiden: Brill.

Van Eyghen, H., Peels, R., and Brink, G. V. D. (2018). The Cognitive Science of Religion, Philosophy, and Theology: A Survey of the Issues. In H. van Eyghen, R. Peels, and G. van den Brink, eds., *New Developments in the Cognitive Science of Religion: The Rationality of Religious Beliefs*. Cham: Springer. 1–15.

van Mastricht, P. (2019). *Faith in the Triune God*. Vol. II of *Theoretical-Practical Theology*. Translated by T. M. Rester. J. R. Beeke, ed. Grand Rapids: Reformation Heritage Books.

Vater, C. A. (2022). *God's Knowledge of the World: Medieval Theories of Divine Ideas from Bonaventure to Ockham*. Washington, DC: Catholic University of America Press.

Visala, A. (2018). Human Cognition and the Image of God. In O. D. Crisp and F. Sanders, eds. *The Christian Doctrine of Humanity: Explorations in Constructive Dogmatics*. Grand Rapids: Zondervan Academic. 91–109.

Ward, G. (2016). *How the Light Gets In: Ethical Life I*. Oxford: Oxford University Press.

Webster, J. (2012). *The Domain of the Word: Scripture and Theological Reason*. London: T&T Clark.

Wolfe, J. (2013). *Heidegger's Eschatology: Theological Horizon's in Martin Heidegger's Early Work*. Oxford: Oxford University Press.

Zahl, S. (2015). On the Affective Salience of Doctrine. *Modern Theology*, 31, 428–444.

Zahl, S. (2021). *The Holy Spirit and Christian Experience*. Oxford: Oxford University Press.

Acknowledgments

This Element has been gestating in my mind for a better part of sixteen years, as I wrestled with the epistemologies of Herman Bavinck and Alvin Plantinga. I'm especially grateful to Simeon Zahl for encouraging me with the work for a potential Element on this topic in this series. I also thank New College, the University of Edinburgh, and the South Carolina Analytic Theology Workshop in Anderson University, SC, for hosting seminar sessions in the summer of 2025 on initial drafts of this work – thanks to Arthur Rankin, Luke Stamps, and Sebastian Bjernegård for providing helpful responses, and for Kimberley Kroll, Rachel Muers, Kegan Shaw, JT Turner, Cory Brock, Marinus de Jong, Joshua Ralston, and participants in the seminars, for their comments along the way. James Eglinton, Scott Swain, and James Anderson also read either the whole or parts of the manuscript and gave invaluable feedback. The anonymous peer-reviewers, as to be expected, helped improve this work in substantial ways. Any shortcomings, of course, remain my responsibility.

I am grateful, as ever, to Reformed Theological Seminary and my colleagues in Washington D.C. for their generosity – again, Scott Redd, Peter Lee, Paul Jeon, Jennifer Patterson, Tommy Keene, and Stephanie DiMaria make for ideal colleagues. Stephanie in particular helped with the formatting of this manuscript for submission. I am also grateful to my research assistant, Isaac Whitney, for his help in proofreading this manuscript.

Thank you to my wife, Indita Probosutedjo, and my dear daughters, Kiandara and Raya Sutanto, for their patience as their father worked long hours working on this and other projects. They are the light that gladdens my heart and serve as reminders of divine mercies.

Christian Doctrine

Rachel Muers
University of Edinburgh

Rachel Muers is Professor of Divinity at the University of Edinburgh. Her publications include *Keeping God's Silence* (2004), *Living for the Future* (2008), and *Testimony: Quakerism and Theological Ethics* (2015). She is co-editor of *Ford's The Modern Theologians: An Introduction to Christian Theology Since 1918*, 4th edition (2024). She is a former president of the Society for the Study of Theology.

Ashley Cocksworth
University of Roehampton

Ashley Cocksworth is Reader in Theology and Practice at the University of Roehampton, UK. He is the author of *Karl Barth on Prayer*; *Prayer: A Guide for the Perplexed*; and (with David F. Ford) *Glorification and the Life of Faith*. His edited volumes include *T&T Clark Handbook of Christian Prayer*; *Karl Barth: Spiritual Writings*; and (with Rachel Muers), *Ford's The Modern Theologians: An Introduction to Christian Theology since 1918*.

Simeon Zahl
University of Cambridge

Simeon Zahl is Professor of Christian Theology at the University of Cambridge and a Fellow of Jesus College.

About the Series

Elements in Christian Doctrine brings creative and constructive thinking in the field of Christian doctrine to a global audience within and beyond the academy. The series demonstrates the vitality of Christian doctrine and its capacity to engage with contemporary questions.

For EU product safety concerns, contact us at Calle de José Abascal, 56–1º,
28003 Madrid, Spain or eugpsr@cambridge.org.

www.ingramcontent.com/pod-product-compliance
Ingram Content Group UK Ltd.
Pitfield, Milton Keynes, MK11 3LW, UK
UKHW021942070625
459283UK00021B/282